Education and economic decline in Britain,
1870 to the 1990s

New Studies in Economic and Social History

Edited for the Economic History Society by
Michael Sanderson
University of East Anglia, Norwich

This series, specially commissioned by the Economic History Society, provides a guide to the current interpretations of the key themes of economic and social history in which advances have recently been made or in which there has been significant debate.

In recent times economic and social history has been one of the most flourishing areas of historical study. This has mirrored the increasing relevance of the economic and social sciences both in a student's choice of career and in forming a society at large more aware of the importance of these issues in their everyday lives. Moreover specialist interests in business, agricultural and welfare history, for example, have themselves burgeoned and there has been an increased interest in the economic development of the wider world. Stimulating as these scholarly developments have been for the specialist, the rapid advance of the subject and the quantity of new publications make it difficult for the reader to gain an overview of particular topics, let alone the whole field.

New Studies in Economic and Social History is intended for students and their teachers. It is designed to introduce them to fresh topics and to enable them to keep abreast of recent writing and debates. All the books in the series are written by a recognised authority in the subject, and the arguments and issues are set out in a critical but unpartisan fashion. The aim of the series is to survey the current state of scholarship, rather than to provide a set of pre-packaged conclusions.

The series has been edited since its inception in 1968 by Professors M. W. Flinn, T. C. Smout and L. A. Clarkson, and is currently edited by Dr Michael Sanderson. From 1968 it was published by Macmillan as Studies in Economic History, and after 1974 as Studies in Economic and Social History. From 1995 New Studies in Economic and Social History is being published on behalf of the Economic History Society by Cambridge University Press. This new series includes some of the titles previously published by Macmillan as well as new titles, and reflects the ongoing development throughout the world of this rich seam of history.

For a full list of titles in print, please see the end of the book.

Education and economic decline in Britain, 1870 to the 1990s

Prepared for the Economic History Society by

Michael Sanderson
University of East Anglia

CAMBRIDGE
UNIVERSITY PRESS

PUBLISHED BY THE PRESS SYNDICATE OF THE UNIVERSITY OF CAMBRIDGE
The Pitt Building, Trumpington Street, Cambridge CB2 1RP, United Kingdom

CAMBRIDGE UNIVERSITY PRESS
The Edinburgh Building, Cambridge CB2 2RU, UK http://www.cup.cam.ac.uk
40 West 20th Street, New York, NY 10011–4211, USA http://www.cup.org
10 Stamford Road, Oakleigh, Melbourne 3166, Australia

© Economic History Society 1999

First published 1999

Printed in the United Kingdom at the University Press, Cambridge

Typeset in Plantin 10/12$\frac{1}{2}$pt   [CE]

A catalogue record for this book is available from the British Library

Library of Congress cataloguing-in-publication data

Sanderson, Michael.
    Education and economic decline in Britain, 1870 to the 1990s / prepared for the Economic History Society by Michael Sanderson.
    p.   cm. – (New studies in economic and social history)
    Includes bibliographical references and index.
    ISBN 0 521 58170 2 (hardback). – ISBN 0 521 588421 1 (paperback)
    1. Education – Economic aspects – Great Britain – History. 2. Great Britain – Economic conditions – 19th century. 3. Great Britain – Economic conditions – 20th century. 4. Educational sociology – Great Britain – History. 5. Education – Great Britain – History. 6. Economic development – Effect of education on – History. I. Economic History Society. II. Title. III. Series.
    LC67.G7S36   1999
    338.4'737'0941–dc21   98–42342 CIP

ISBN 0 521 58170 2 hardback
ISBN 0 521 58842 1 paperback

Contents

Acknowledgements

This book has benefited from many influences in recent years where the themes relevant to its subject have been discussed. It is a pleasure to recall and acknowledge Professor N. F. R. Crafts' conference at Oxford on British long-run economic performance resulting in the papers of the Oxford Review of Economic Policy in 1988, also Gabriel Tortella's conferences in Valencia and Leuven on education and economic development and valuable conversations there with Professor Derek Aldcroft. Jean Pierre Dormois' conference in Montpellier on the roots of decline was especially valuable and further enlivened by discussions with Dr Correlli Barnett CBE. All these helped to stimulate and enrich my interest in this subject, for which I am grateful.

I am glad to acknowledge Her Majesty's Stationery Office in Norwich for permission to reproduce the cover photograph of a Secondary Technical School from *The New Secondary Education* 1947.

I am chiefly indebted to Professor Sidney Pollard FBA who read the original proposal, the draft and revised scripts and whose valuable expertise and advice have greatly benefited the final version.

Glossary and abbreviations

BTEC	Business and Technician Education Council
CAT	College of Advanced Technology
CBI	Confederation of British Industry
Clarendon Schools	The public schools investigated by Lord Clarendon's Commission (1861–4). Eton, Winchester, Westminster, Charterhouse, Harrow, Rugby, Shrewsbury, Merchant Taylor's St Paul's
CPVE	Certificate of Pre-Vocational Education
CTC	City Technology College
DES	Department of Education and Science
DSIR	Department of Scientific and Industrial Research
ET	Employment Training
GCSE	General Certificate of Secondary Education
GDP	Gross Domestic Product
GNP	Gross National Product
GNVQ	General National Vocational Qualification
HMC	Headmasters' Conference
HNC	Higher National Certificate
IQ	Intelligence Quotient
ITB	Industrial Training Board
JTS	Junior Technical School
LEA	Local Education Authority
MBA	Master of Business Administration
NCVQ	National Council for Vocational Qualifications
NVQ	National Vocational Qualification
ONC	Ordinary National Certificate
STS	Secondary Technical School
TEC	Training and Enterprise Council
TH	Technische Hochschule
TVEI	Technical and Vocational Education Initiative
UGC	University Grants Committee

VET	Vocational Education and Training
YOP	Youth Opportunities Programme
YT	Youth Training
YTS	Youth Training Scheme

Introduction

In 1882 Sir Bernhard Samuelson, after a lengthy investigation of education, science and industry, concluded that 'the Englishman has yet to learn that an extended and systematic education is now a necessary preliminary to the fullest development of industry.'[1] A century later in 1986 Sir Bryan Nicholson of the Manpower Services Commission put it more succinctly: 'we are a bunch of thickies'.[2]

In the last hundred and thirty years or so Britain has steadily declined from its economic position as the 'workshop of the world' to that of a low-ranking laggard European power. Our share of world manufactured exports has fallen from around 45 per cent in 1875 to 30 per cent by 1913, 20 per cent by 1939, 25 per cent by the early 1950s, before slumping to 5 per cent by 1994. As this happened so we were overtaken successively by other powers. In 1870 our Gross Domestic Product per head was second only to Australia in the world. By 1913 we had been overtaken by the United States and Belgium in addition. Fewer than forty years later, by 1950, Canada, Switzerland and Sweden had also surpassed us and Germany overtook us in the 1950s. Then the decline was headlong in the 1960s and 1970s so that by 1976 Norway, Japan, France, Denmark, Finland, Austria, Netherlands, Belgium (which had temporarily fallen behind but once again overtaken us) had all joined those front runners ahead of us (Aldcroft, 1982 citing Maddison). Only Italy lay behind, but by 1985 that country too had surpassed Britain in GDP per head. By 1996, in spite of Thatcherite aims to reverse decline we had sunk to fifteenth in World Economic

[1] 1882 XXIX Royal Commission on Technical Instruction (Samuelson) p. 525.
[2] *The Daily Telegraph*, 21 March 1986.

Forum rankings, sixteenth in GDP in the OECD and nineteenth in Institute of Management Development ratings.

This decline is, of course, relative. It goes without saying that Britain is far richer now than in the 1870s or even in the 1970s. In fact our GDP per capita has increased six or seven-fold between 1870 and 1989 (Johnson, 1994 p. 3 citing Angus Maddison). Also our growth rate has not declined but remained remarkably steady at around 2 per cent for the periods 1872–1913, 1924–37 and 1950–83 (Supple, 1994). It was beyond belief that a small off-shore island with limited resources could remain the world's economic leader for two centuries without challenge. The wonder is that we held our position so long until after 1945. The relative decline has been rapid only since the 1960s and its perception is made the sharper by our corresponding awareness of the loss of our once Great Power status since the Second World War. Yet it is fair to regard this as a long-term change. It suits politicians to emphasise the long-term, deep-seated nature of decline in order to draw attention from the sharpness of the fall from around 1960; to do so shifts some of the responsibility away from themselves back to some remote period of the past back in the nineteenth century. Hence the extraordinary popularity among businessmen and Margaret Thatcher's ministers in the 1980s of Martin Wiener's argument that the industrial spirit had been declining in England since as early as the 1850s. There is also a long tradition of attributing this decline to defects of education. This too conveniently passes the blame not only to the past but on to teachers, schools and universities and consequently away from the City, the entrepreneurs, the Treasury and politicians (Raven, 1989). There are vested interests and loaded debates here.

The purpose of this book is not to survey all the possible reasons for decline nor all aspects of the history of education in this time. Rather, we are concerned to take up the issue of education's supposed part – or not – in the decline and focus on those issues where education has been seen to fail the needs of the economy. We are also especially interested in those areas where there has been some debate between those who would emphasise or deny education's contribution to or culpability for Britain's diminished economic state.

1
Literacy and schooling, 1870–1914

Let us begin by considering the condition of literacy. In the period from 1870 to 1913 Britain achieved virtually total literacy in the workforce. As measured by the capacity to sign one's name literacy rose from 80 per cent in 1870 to 97 per cent by 1900 (Stone, 1969; Baines, 1981). Even among the criminal classes only 19.3 per cent were still illiterate by 1898 (Harris, 1993 p. 213). In Scotland literacy rose from 90 per cent in 1870 to 98 per cent in 1900 for men and from 80 per cent to 97 per cent for women over the same period (Anderson, 1997, p. 39). David Vincent has analysed the trend to mass total literacy by social groups (Vincent, 1989 p. 97). See table 1.1.

The rise in literacy is seen across the spectrum of occupations. Whereas only social classes 1 and 2 were almost all literate by the 1870s this position was achieved for most of the rest by 1904–9 and was virtually total for all groups by 1914. For some the advance was remarkable, especially for metal workers and miners who made 25 and 52 percentage point gains from the 1870s to 1914. Textile workers and miners, the notorious literacy laggards of the Industrial Revolution before 1830, achieved total literacy by 1914. So it was for their womenfolk where brides are considered by the occupation of their fathers (Vincent, 1989 p. 102). See table 1.2.

Various factors lay behind this. There was a gradual extension of compulsory education (Lowndes, 1969). The Forster Act of 1870 created the School Boards which were units of local government dedicated to building and running secular elementary schools. In Scotland there were School Boards from 1872 to 1918 likewise to provide a single local authority and plug gaps in universal provision.

Table 1.1 Occupational literacy of men by social class

period	1	2	handicraft	textiles	metal	miners	4	5
1874–9	100	96	90	84	75	47	79	56
1884–9	100	96	94	93	88	70	92	71
1894–9	100	98	99	86	95	88	97	86
1904–9	100	100	99	100	100	97	99	97
1914	100	100	98	100	100	99	99	99

Table 1.2 Literacy of brides by fathers' social class

period	1	2	handicraft	textiles	metal	miners	4	5
1874–9	95	91	74	69	65	43	79	69
1884–9	100	92	79	83	82	66	87	82
1894–9	100	99	93	86	89	92	93	95
1904–9	100	99	98	96	98	98	97	97
1914	100	98	99	100	98	99	98	97

They were given powers to make by-laws to compel attendance from the ages of five to ten and by 1876 a half of the whole child population was subject to this compulsion and an even higher 84 per cent of children living in boroughs. In 1876 Lord Sandon's Act prohibited the employment of children under the age of ten living within two miles of a school. It also imposed on parents the duty of ensuring that the child should receive 'efficient elementary instruction in reading writing and arithmetic'. It did not compel the sending of a child to school (unless they were already under by-laws to that effect) but doing so was the easiest way for parents to ensure the provision of 'efficient instruction'. This was soon followed by A. J. Mundella's Act of 1880 which obliged all School Boards which had not already done so, to enforce compulsory attendance for all children between the ages of five and ten. A further act raised the school leaving age to eleven from 1894. The leaving age was raised to twelve in 1899 without exception. Then an act of 1900 gave School Boards leave to make by-laws raising it further to fourteen in their area, though the decision to have fourteen as the national school leaving age did not come about until the Fisher Act of 1918.

All this was reinforced by School Attendance Officers ('kidcoppers') who could take an erring parent to court. A more subtle interim stage would be for a child whose attendance was poor to be threatened with expulsion from his nearby school, forcing him to attend a more distant one – still under compulsion. The fear of this extra harassing journey was often enough to bring the recalcitrant parent to heel. Prosecutions for non-attendance reached a peak in the mid 1880s, which suggests that parents did not take long to understand the resolve of the state in this matter and that they had to comply with it. Accordingly school attendance rose from 1.2 million in 1860 to 4.7 million by 1900 and enrolment rates of five to nine-year-olds rose from 57.3 per cent in 1871 to 82.6 per cent by 1896 and presumably the totality by 1900 (Mitch, 1992 p. 188).

Education also became more pleasing and acceptable to children and parents. Not least, it became free of charge. Curiously, in the 1880s education though compulsory was not free, which made collecting fee pence from poor and unwilling parents difficult (Rubinstein, 1969). This anomaly was removed in 1891 when a fee grant of ten shillings a head was introduced, making elementary education virtually free. Fees in elementary schools were finally abolished altogether by the Fisher Act of 1918. Secondly, what the children learnt was likely to be of use to them. The system of 'payment by results' from 1862 to 1897 imposed in effect a kind of national curriculum defined by the Codes. These were lists of subjects on which schools could gain grant income when their pupils passed the appropriate examination. The initial Revised Code of 1862 undoubtedly had adverse effects in discouraging wider education beyond the 3 Rs, which was accordingly neglected. The 1862 Code led to mechanical systems of teaching, a fall in the education grant, a decrease in teachers and an increase in class sizes, from all of which education as a whole suffered. On the other hand it did have the salutary effect of making teachers focus on 'cash earning' subjects – reading a short passage from a newspaper, writing from dictation and doing arithmetic. The more mentally enriching history, geography and science were added from 1875. The Code induced teachers to ensure that all children had reached an acceptable level of literacy and this was made the more effective by a sharp rise in elementary school attendance to over a million by 1866.

Thirdly there is evidence that most children actually enjoyed their education and this enhanced their receptivity to learning. Jonathan Rose finds that 66.2 per cent of children in this period (including 72.5 per cent of girls) had positively enjoyed their schooling and only 14.7 per cent positively disliked it (Rose, 1993). This result is a useful corrective to the impression that working-class education was a soulless affair of drudgery enforced by harsh discipline. The environment of education also became more attractive. It was the job of the new School Boards from 1870 to build and run new schools and a massive school building programme created 3.7 million new places between 1870 and 1895. These ranged from intimate village schools to great three-decker Board Schools, light, spacious and airy, such as those built by E. R. Robson for the London School Board. Reading matter too made learning more attractive to those newly acquiring literacy. In the 1860s Macmillan, Routledge, Nelson and Longman set up juvenile departments and by the 1880s 900 new juvenile books were being published annually and 15 boys period-icals and 'penny dreadfuls' (Springhall, 1994). Some of the readers of these would have graduated to *The Daily Mail* 1896, *The Daily Express* 1900, and *The Daily Herald* 1912, which were all buoyed by the rising literacy of their new readership at this time.

A further element in improving elementary education was the increase in state finance. Just as this had helped to drive up literacy rates in the 1840 to 1870 period, so it was still playing an important role between 1870 and 1914. Mitch has shown that the subsidies per scholar rose from 15.50 shillings in 1870 to 58.18 in 1899. From 1891 state subsidies rose sharply to offset the declining contribution of fees such that total real expenditure per pupil rose from 22.95 shillings in 1870 to 59.74 shillings by 1899 (Mitch, 1986). Much of this increased subsidy went to reduce pupil–teacher ratios, accompanied by an increase in the real wages of teachers, which must have improved teaching effectiveness and added to greater feelings of satisfaction in the classroom – points detected by Rose (1993).

E. G. West, by contrast, focuses not on the achievements of the post 1870 period but sees it as a period of retardation in elemen-tary education (West, 1975). He argues that the increase in state funding, local and national, during the School Board era of 1870 to 1902 was offset by a decline in private funding which had been part of the 1833–1870 expansion. Accordingly, while elementary education expenditure rose from 1 per cent of GNP in 1833 to 1.10 by 1858, it declined to 1.06 by 1882. This 1882 figure compares modestly with 1.10 per cent for the United States and 1.6 per cent for Germany both in 1880. Moreover Britain is the only country where the proportion of the GNP spent on elementary education fell between the 1850s and 1880s whereas other countries show a rise. He suggests that this decline in the proportion of educational expenditure may have contributed to the economic slowdown around 1900. It is an intriguing argument and has the merit of reminding us just how fast was the expansion of elementary education between 1840 and 1870 and of establishing that our expenditure on elementary education as a percentage of GNP was consistent with other major competitor countries. However it is difficult to relate this to economic slowdown around 1900 when the education system was delivering virtually one hundred per cent literacy and enrolment even for the most previously illiterate of the labour force by that time. If there really had been a fall in expenditure, enrolment, and literacy between 1870 and 1914 and a less literate labour force by the 1900s undermining the economy, then the West argument would have greater force.

How relevant was the state of literacy and elementary education for the economy ? In the early nineteenth century there was only limited demand for literate labour especially in the new textile industries. However David Mitch suggests that the Victorian economy 'changed course ... so as to increase the demands for educated labour. Although a worker did not have to be literate to run a spinning mule in a cotton factory during the early nineteenth century he did in order to run a railroad locomotive or deliver a letter in the last half of the nineteenth century' (Mitch, 1992 p. 37). Schooling could enhance job performance by providing literacy which may have direct relevance to the task – keeping accounts, reading and writing instructions and reports and so forth. It was equally valuable in inculcating social discipline, promoting an orderly mind and facilitating urban living with its signs, advertisements for jobs and housing, and enabling intelligent engagement in religious, political and recreational activity. In occupational change between 1851 and 1891 the percentage of male workers in jobs where literacy was required or likely to be useful rose from 28.4 per cent to 37.2 and those in jobs where literacy was unlikely to have been useful fell from 47 to 37 per cent. The corresponding figures for women were a rise from 8.6 to 15.4 and a fall from 33.4 to 25.5. There was a clear premium on literacy in workers' wages though falling slightly as the supply of literate male workers increased even faster than the demand for them. For women Mitch considers the premium would have been higher due to new opportunities in school teaching. In a specific instance Lady Florence Bell found that in her husband's iron works in Middlesbrough in the 1900s literacy related quite closely to earnings. The median weekly wage of the six workmen who could not read was 23 shillings a week, that for eighteen men who could read but did not was 27 shillings, and that for the forty who could and did read was 36 shillings (Bell, 1907).

Linked with prospects for enhanced earnings for the literate was the greater likelihood of upward social mobility. The rise in literacy for the upwardly socially mobile suggested that literacy was increasingly valued in job requirements. Mitch suggests that 'on average literate workers from all social origins were more likely to move into higher status occupations than their illiterate counterparts' (Mitch, 1992 p. 36). Although his specific evidence relates to the 1840–70 period he attributes his finding generally to 'the second half of the nineteenth century' (Mitch, 1992, p. 41).

If education and literacy gave advantages to a labour force seeking advanced earning and social mobility there was the reciprocal point that employment was diminishing as a barrier to education. In the early nineteenth century the opportunities for child work in factories and field acted as a great diversion from school, especially as parents had to take into account not only the costs of schooling but foregone child earnings. After 1870 this was much less so. The percentage of children aged between 10 and 14 who were employed fell from 32.1 of boys and 20.4 per cent of girls in 1870 down to 18.3 per cent of boys and 10.4 per cent of girls by 1911. This was partly due to the diminishing importance of textiles and agriculture, the chief child employers, in the share of the labour force. Also the progressive raising of the school leaving age, potentially to fourteen after 1900 imposed this.

Although we may be fairly satisfied with the achievement of virtually total literacy and its relevance to the economy yet we should remember that merely the capacity to sign one's name is not perfect literacy. But more importantly we should also be aware that perfect literacy, as a schoolteacher might understand it, was far from necessary for effective job performance even in skilled jobs. My great grandfather was a brass founder and metallurgist at the Horwich railway workshops in the 1880s. He needed literacy to keep records of his 'receipts' or formulae for different types of metal. He wrote a fine hand yet he spelled 'two handfuls' as 'tow hanfuls' and 'Britannia' (metal) as 'Brotannia'. Likewise my grandfather in another line of the family grew asparagus for the Blackpool holiday trade before the First World War. Yet he called and spelled it 'sparrer (sparrow) grass'. Neither man's capacity to produce excellent products was impeded by their limitations of spelling and correct English. It is more important to be able to make the product than to spell the word that represents it – they had their priorities right.

If the rise of literacy was uncontentiously desirable for the formation of the labour force, the changes in post-elementary education in the 1900s remain disputed. In the 1890s post-elementary education was in a confused and illegal state. No formal leaving age had been set by the 1870 Act, children passed through seven standards and when they had completed them it was assumed that they would leave at the earliest opportunity – at ten from 1876. In practice about half the children reached standard seven. But there were always children who wanted to stay on at school beyond that. They were catered for in extra class-rooms annexed to the main elementary schools and called 'higher tops' or in sizeable towns new higher grade schools would be built expressly to gather children for post elementary work. This was of doubtful legality, since what was in effect secondary education was being financed under the 1870 Act, which was supposed to cover only elementary education.

Sir George Kekewich, the senior civil servant at the Education Department allowed this indefensible situation to continue, since he saw it as a way of providing the working classes with a kind of secondary education by stealth. But others had different ideas. His junior colleagues, Sir Michael Sadler and Sir Robert Morant, were coming to the view that the entire system needed to be restructured so that elementary education would be followed by secondary schooling (for some but not all) thus providing administrative clarity, legality and an organised flow from one level to the other. Sadler and Morant were influenced by the conclusions of the 1895 Royal Commission on Secondary Education and by studies of continental systems with their clear stratification of educational levels. The illegality of the existing British system was verified by the Cockerton Judgement of 1899 which declared illegal all School Board rate spending on post-elementary education. This opened the way for the reorganisation of the system under Sir Robert Morant who succeeded Kekewich at the new Board of Education.

There are two aspects of Morant's policies which had implications for the formation both of the social structure and the labour force and which remain contentious. Firstly the higher grade schools were abolished. Accordingly, some children who might have proceeded from elementary school to higher grade school had their education restricted to elementary schools with a leaving age, from 1900, of thirteen. Instead, greater opportunities were provided by the development of genuine grammar schools to be created by new Local Education Authorities under the Education Act of 1902. These admitted children from elementary schools on scholarships won by the competitive 'eleven plus' examination. From 1907 Morant required the grammar schools to set aside a quarter of their places for scholarship winners from the elementary schools and by 1913 34.8 per cent of grammar school pupils were free-place scholarship winners. The other children in grammar schools would be from a higher social background who would enter by paying fees. The key question was whether this was an advance or whether Morant was denying advantages to the working classes which they had enjoyed before, thereby perpetuating the highly stratified social structure of Edwardian England. The figures suggest that a more fluid system was being created. There were eighty-five higher grade schools in 1902 but 736 new grammar schools by 1910. Secondly, whereas in 1897 the sons of skilled artisans and unskilled workers made up only 9 per cent of grammar school and 40 per cent of higher grade pupils, yet by 1913 these groups made up 20.6 per cent of grammar school pupils (Reeder, 1987). There were far more secondary schools by 1913 and the working class made up a far higher proportion of grammar schools by the later date. Gains must have been evident quantitatively and certainly qualitatively and Reeder is confident that this was so by the 1920s. Morant was a man devoted not to the perpetuation of a rigid social structure but to social mobility and the circulation of élites. He believed in the necessity of an élite of which he saw himself a part. Yet he was clear that the same families could not generation after generation be relied upon to supply that élite. Talent had to be raised from the lower social classes through different educational levels, ladders and scholarships. It was under Morant that LEA scholarships began not only enabling elementary school pupils to enter grammar schools but also to move from grammar school to university.

The criticism is also levelled against Morant that he forced ideals of liberal education on the state system and was hostile to technical education. Morant was a product of Winchester and Oxford and the grammar schools were to be municipal reflections of the values they embodied. His regulation of 1904 required grammar schools to devote eight hours a week to English, history, geography and languages and if two languages were studied one had to be Latin. His emphasis on Latin may be taken in two ways. On the one hand he can be criticised for his curricular conservatism, perpetuating and boosting a classical tradition more appropriate to a landed ruling class and the clergy while marginalising the more modern and scientific subjects needed by business and professional men of the new century. On the other hand it can be seen as part of his concern about social mobility. To oblige working-class scholarship pupils in new LEA grammar schools to study Latin was not a perverse irrelevance; it opened the doors not merely to local civic universities but to Oxford and Cambridge and the careers that could follow.

More controversially Morant was concerned to prevent a small number of grammar schools from pursuing curricula heavily biased towards science (Vlaemincke in Evans and Summerfield, 1990). Some grammar schools at the turn of the century had sought to increase their incomes by accepting funds from the Science and Art Department in return for pursuing a science curriculum. Morant regarded this as unbalancing the diet and his

1904 regulations were intended as a corrective, though Cane considers that he overestimated the problem (Cane, 1959). Morant's supposed anti-technical bias is belied by his other policies in the 1900s. Morant had travelled on the Continent investigating education in other countries and was probably better informed about European systems of technical education than almost anybody in England. His report on French technical schools, the *écoles primaires supérieures,* influenced his attitudes and contains some of the most passionate writing in favour of craftsmanship and the importance of the technical training of the young penned in these years (Sanderson, 1996). He carried this into action with his creation of the Junior Technical Schools in the modification of the Regulations of 1905/6 which led to their full Regulations of 1913. He also sanctioned the Central Schools of some cities in the 1900s which provided a commercial alternative to the academic grammar school and the Junior Technical School. His concern to distance the grammar school from these more practical forms can be seen in this context. But Vlaemincke's strictures do have some justification since this small number of schools might have presaged the technical-grammar school (which some JTSs eventually became in the 1960s) and which would have been a useful part of a diversified secondary education for the century. On balance one may set on one side Morant's emphasis on social mobility through the new accessible grammar school and on early technical training through the JTS. These undoubtedly benefited the economy. On the other side others may emphasise his stress on liberal education and his blind spot over the nascent grammar-technical school. It is interesting that one of the earliest conversations between R. A. Butler, as incoming President of the Board of Education in 1941, and his officials (many of whom had served with Morant), had been on the the the subject of Morant. He casts a long shadow.

Scotland's experiences partly reflected and mirrored those of England. An act of 1887 had allowed School Boards to create technical schools but this opportunity remained unused (Anderson, 1983 p. 210). It seems a pity that a country so proud of its engineering and apprenticeships denied itself a useful form of pre-apprenticeship training such as the French enjoyed. The School Boards in Scotland lasted until 1918 and it was only then that education was transferred to county and city education authorities

(Anderson, 1997). Yet 1903 was a turning point for the Scots as 1902 was in England. There too there was more concern to create a differentiation of types of secondary schools by social function, similar to what Morant was doing. But, whereas Morant was cutting back an overemphasis on science in some English secondary schools, the Scots were concerned to rebalance the arts orientation of Scottish schools with more science (Anderson, 1983 pp. 223–30). Both systems were concerned to modify in ways appropriate for the industrial societies they inhabited.

2
Was technical education to blame?

A great deal of controversy has been associated with the question of defects of scientific and technical education and their culpability for Britain's supposed poor economic performance before 1914. This chapter will consider the arguments of those who hold this view.

This was certainly the opinion held by many contemporaries and it arose primarily from a cluster of events around 1870. In 1867 British industrialists displayed their wares at the International Exposition in Paris and won only ten of the ninety classes. This was in contrast to the Great Exhibition in 1851 when British manufacturers won most of the prizes. A commentator noted 'by that Exhibition we were rudely awakened and thoroughly alarmed ... we were beaten on nearly all those points on which we have prided ourselves' (Ahlstrom, 1982 citing J. Scott Russel). The Royal Society of Arts sent artisans to Paris to report and they too observed 'the general deficiency of the technical knowledge of our best workmen' (Sanderson, 1996). Subsequent Paris expositions in 1878, 1889, 1900 drove the message home. In the next year, 1868, Matthew Arnold's report on Prussian education drew our attention to the superiority of that country which had a systematised education providing universal literacy, scientific instruction and a military strength that underlay its nation building by war. The Paris Exhibition of 1867 led to a long sequence of investigations into science, industry and technical education by Bernhard Samuelson in 1868, the Duke of Devonshire 1870–5, Samuelson again in 1884 and the Royal Commission on the Great Depression in 1886. From 1895 the Education Department and subsequent Board of Education ran an Office of Special Inquiries and Reports producing dozens of reports about aspects of education in other countries which were by comparison critical of defects and arrangements at home. There was scarcely a year when somebody was not investigating and reporting on supposed deficiencies in British education and there was scarcely a topic which received such a barrage of repetitive attention in these years. It is hardly surprising that subsequent historians have echoed these concerns.

The concern was exacerbated and even exaggerated by the Victorian's perceptions of declining industrial pre-eminence. We have seen some of the figures earlier. Most late Victorians and Edwardians would have been unaware of the statistics but would have been troubled by the rhetoric. They spoke of a 'Great Depression' from the 1870s to the 1890s, a falling in profits and employment and a slackness of trade. The Royal Commission on the Great Depression devoted its third volume specifically to education, drawing a connection in the public mind between education and decline. They would also have been conscious of the waves of imports some 'Made in Germany' – toys, optical glass, electrical goods, dyestuffs and pharmaceuticals and others part of the 'American Invasion' – shoes, bicycles, machine tools. Above all there was the problem of dyestuffs. W. H. Perkin had produced the first coal tar dye, mauve, in 1856, but the industry was lost to the Germans for our lack of education and expertise in organic chemistry. The Germans consequently achieved world domination in this product with 85 per cent of world production by 1913. The Jubilee of Perkin's discovery coincided with the creation of Imperial College (opened 1907) and occasioned days of correspondence in *The Times* recriminating about the loss of the industry, the educational defects that had occasioned this and the determination through institutions like Imperial College, that it should not happen again. No other issue so convinced the Victorians and Edwardians of the connection between education and industry and it has been a major plank in the historians' case since (Wrigley, 1986).

Contemporaries saw further links between education and the economy through the debate on protection and free trade. Free Traders like Lyon Playfair argued that if Britain were to remain without tariffs, as he advocated, then it would be self defeating unless British industry were made as efficient as that of countries from which we imported. Education for economic efficiency was the only true protection. On the other hand Sir Philip Magnus of the City and Guilds similarly linked his opinions about education with a contrary preference for protection. He argued that in many industries countries had no particular natural advantages in manufacturing and exporting as the classical economists had held. On the contrary, by the later nineteenth century it was quite possible by state support for science and education to create industries from chemistry and electrical physics based on creatable and educable expertise rather than natural endowments. These could be developed behind tariffs, as the Germans had done with their dyestuffs and electrical industries. But the protection in itself would add greater urgency to the need for education, otherwise such industries shielded from competition would sink into lethargy. Both tariff reformers and free traders believed in the vital role of technical education and argued from different standpoints that there was more need for it.

Another argument is that Britain was held back in its attitudes to technical education by the legacy of the limited contribution of formal education to the Industrial Revolution of the eighteenth and early nineteenth centuries. The textile industries thrived with a workforce of very low literacy, the two enfeebled universities of Oxford and Cambridge offered nothing to industrial science, and there was no technical education structure for the working classes before the Mechanics Institutes of the 1820s which failed to fulfil their technical purpose for lack of literacy among their working class clients. There was a preference for practical learning on the job, starting in early adolescence if not before, and it served the country well at that time. It was not surprising that such attitudes – that education had not mattered much for industrialisation in the past and probably did not in the present – lasted well into the nineteenth century. Middle-aged businessmen in the 1880s would have been brought up with the outlook of the 1830s, 40s and 50s.

Moreover it can be argued that such attitudes would be reinforced by Britain's ample labour supply. This was the result of steadily rising population and especially the migration of poor agricultural labourers made unemployed or impoverished by the agricultural depression of the 1870s to 90s. They sought jobs in the factories, mines, docks and building sites, glutting the labour force and keeping wages low. This in turn inhibited the need to replace short supply or expensive labour with machinery as in the United States. In the United States labour shortage and rapid turnover of immigrant labour had occasioned resort to substitute mechanisation, machine tools and mass production as the skill lacking in the mind and hand of the immigrant labourer had to be put into the machine (Habbakuk, 1962). This in turn generated a respect for the engineer, the mechanic and his training. In England by contrast there was more labour, large stable communities of embodied skill, more poor men who would hew and hump with no prospect of escaping to farms of their own. There was less mechanisation, more reliance on physical labour, late acceptance of machine tools and mechanisation of coal mines for example. Gray and Turner found for 26 industries that output per worker per year in the United States was twice that of the United Kingdom (Gray and Turner, 1916 pp. 136–9). England was almost unique in Europe (with Denmark and the Netherlands) in allowing free importation of agricultural goods during the agricultural depression and the surplus labour that created, moving off the land, may have influenced attitudes to technical training.

The need for more technical education was increased by the supposed 'decline of apprenticeship' which was a common concern and phrase of the 1890s and 1900s. The introduction of machine tools began to change the training of craftsmen mechanics who used to serve a seven-year apprenticeship learning their skill with a master. The new machines broke down the hand work of the all-round skilled mechanic into specialised parts which could be done on machines by the semi-skilled. The use of interchangeable parts allowed greater tolerances while semi-skilled assemblers of engineering parts usurped the role of skilled fitters. The role of the apprentice was being degraded to cheap labour. Yet paradoxically higher levels of skill were required in setting and supervising machines. As apprenticeship was ceasing to give an all-round training so there was more need for formal technical education to replace what was diminishingly provided on the job (Knox, 1986; More, 1980).

A major element in the criticism of the defects of British education was a belief in the superiority of that of the Germans. It is expressed in the classic view of David Landes who refers to 'an enormous gap between British and German achievements in this area (i.e. education in relation to industry)' (Landes, 1969 p. 340). Many of the leading Victorian advocates of technical education had studied in Germany or visited the country to investigate its education system as an exemplar which England might follow. At various points the Prussian, and then German system from 1870, seemed to be ahead. Following the defeat of Prussia by Napoleon at Jena in 1806 the Humboldt reforms introduced from 1808 compulsory elementary education for 6 to 14 year olds in the *Volksschulen*. These were staffed by state trained and, from 1810, certificated teachers eventually spread through 155 teacher training colleges by 1905. The outcome was virtually universal literacy from the early nineteenth century onwards. Above that were Trade Continuation Schools (*Fortbildungschulen*) increasing from 435 in 1870 to 1874 in 1906. These took children full time from the ages of 12 to 14 or part time 14 to 18 for those in work. These continued general literacy and numeracy education with trade skills related to employment. For adults there were *Fachschulen* training foremen, lower managers and self-employed craftsmen. Then at the culmination of the technical track were the ten *Technische Hochschulen*, technological universities, usually in major industrial cities relating their studies to the specialisms of their area. They included Stuttgart for automobile engineering, Chemnitz for textiles, Kiel for naval architecture and, most famous of all, Charlottenburg in Berlin for electrical engineering (Locke, 1984).

As well as the technical track there was also the academic one. Much of this, the academic *Gymnasien* secondary schools and the universities, were much the same as English grammar and public schools and Oxford and Cambridge. But as regards service to industry two features were regarded as distinctively superior. Firstly the Germans had developed a wide spectrum of types of secondary school beyond the academic *Gymnasium*. These ranged from the *Realgymnasium* and *Realschulen* of various levels all including increasing amounts of practical, technical and commercial training the further distanced they were from the classics and pure science of the *Gymnasium*. This impressed English reformers of the 1900s who sought to remodel English secondary education on similarly stratified though simplified lines (grammar school, central school, junior technical school). Accordingly German education did not sharply divide youth into the academically able and residual failures but more effectively sought to develop commercial and technical capabilities in the non-academic teenager. This has always been a strength of the German system in the nineteenth century no less than today. The second undoubted superiority of the Germans was their university chemistry. The Germans were pre-eminent in organic chemistry which underpinned their fortes in the dyestuffs and pharmaceutical industries. Research was institutionalised with research professors like Hoffmann, Bayer and Kekulé running departments with doctoral research students (unknown in England before 1914) supplying expertise and personnel to the major chemical firms – BASF, Agfa, Hochst and Bayer. These features that impressed contemporaries like Haldane and Sadler continue to impress historians now (Barnett, 1986). Germany also had a more positive attitude to the state finance of education in support of national industry. By 1900 Germany spent 12.3 million marks on state funding for science and technology departments in universities compared with England's two million (Berghoff and Moller, 1994). There was also no doubt that the German system could produce the numbers and consequently had larger stocks of educated personnel. In 1913 Germany had 27,564 students in its universities and 16,568 in the THs in 1910 (say 44,000 on the eve of the War) (Lundgreen, 1984, Locke, 1984 p. 34) compared with 26,711 for the whole of Britain. Also as regards engineering specifically Locke notes that 'The German technical institutes had three times as many engineering students as the English civic universities had on the eve of the War ... there were only 1,129 students of engineering in all the universities of England and Wales in 1913' (Locke 1984 p. 51). There were 19,581 members of the *Verein Deutscher Ingenieure* in 1910 (Locke, 1984 p. 34) while Ahlstrom regards the entire stock of engineers in Germany with higher education in 1914 as 65,202 but only 48,000 in Britain in 1921 (Ahlstrom, 1982). In the chemical industry Aldcroft finds 1,500 trained chemists in the British chemical industry which compared poorly with the 5,500 in the German industry in 1910 (Aldcroft, 1975). The greater the admiration for German education and industry before 1914 the greater seemed to be the defects of our own system – its late developing literacy, lack of technical training for teenagers and diversification of secondary schools, low stock of scientists, limited government involvement and backwardness in areas of chemistry.

There was a pretty universal view that whatever the rights and wrongs of education the gravest fault lay with employers who were too reluctant to employ educated men. Sir William Ramsay lamented that although the universities could produce good chemists yet 'the demand for such men is not keeping up with the supply, manufacturers are not as yet sufficiently alive to the necessity of employing chemists' (Sanderson, 1972 p. 117). Henry Armstrong likewise noted in the 1890s that 'so far as chemistry was concerned ... manufacturers were still not alive to the need of employing people with technical knowledge ... we have lost the chemical industry not because we had not the chemists but because the manufacturers would not employ them' (Eyre, 1958 pp. 119, 151). Indeed of all chemistry graduates working around 1900, 70–75 per cent of them were employed in teaching (Cardwell, 1957). A similar distortion was seen in Leicestershire where students intended for technical education went into offices instead, 'here one has to note an unexpected result of the policy of encouraging "technical" education. Instead of producing technologists and technicians the effect of the scholarship scheme, in Leicestershire at any rate, was to swell the ranks of the white collar professions.' Seaborne sees lack of employer demand as the root of the problem and finds that 'the movement towards technical education was not developed to the full because many industrialists were less concerned with modernisation than with expanding imperial markets in traditional products' (Seaborne, 1968). In engineering Sir Philip Magnus, the Director of the City and Guilds of London reflecting on an experience in 1899, found that 'there existed a feeling at that time that however serviceable technical instruction might be to managers and masters it was of very little use to the workmen engaged in great industrial occupations ... this contention I had frequently to combat' (Magnus, 1910). Gray and Turner also strongly put the blame squarely on the refusal of employers to value education. In their view it was irrelevant for manufacturers to claim that the products of universities and technical colleges were useless to them, supply follows demand and if manufacturers had pressed for such men and remunerated them adequately then they would have got them. They roundly lambasted 'the manufacturer (who) having been seldom educated in scientific knowledge in the days of his boyhood, relied mainly on antiquated methods and sometimes regarded the academic professor as a product of fossilised humanity' (Gray and Turner, 1916 pp. 106, 66–7). This finds a modern echo in the views of Peter Payne who finds that 'there was a failure of industrial entrepreneurship' to develop new technologies and new high productivity industries and part of this was their lack of demand for education, for 'they did not realise what they were missing' (Payne, 1990).

Why should this have been so? There was the cultural lag hinted at by Gray and Turner, that many businessmen would not have received much scientific education in their own boyhoods and so did not value it in others a generation or so later. There was still the preference for the 'practical man' who had learnt his business on the job in workshop and counting house (Barnett, 1985). Employers who had come through this route themselves would prefer it for their employees. This would be so for employers risen from the ranks of workmen. Paradoxically it would also be so if they had been sent to a public school as part of the social enhancement of the family. There they would have acquired little appreciation of science before returning to a family firm for 'on the job' training to prepare them for management in the firm they would ultimately direct. Also Aldcroft suggests that employers were generally more concerned to keep wages low rather than raise productivity (Aldcroft, 1975). This may have been a response to ample labour supplies referred to earlier. In any case employers would have realised that any expansion of technical education would entail increased expenditure and hence higher taxes and rates which would fall on them. Quintin Hogg's daughter reckoned that technical education was five times more expensive than ordinary schooling; it was a rough and ready estimate but sufficiently alarming for potential cost bearers (Hogg, 1904). In London the lack of employer interest was attributed to the multiplicity of small building, metal working, furniture, printing and clothing firms who could rely on 'an endless influx of skilled labour from the provinces sucked in by the higher pay' (Saint, 1989). In such circumstances the reliance on immigrant labour diminished the urgency to train especially since the training by one firm might be likewise poached by another of similar size and standing. At a higher level Paul Robertson finds the provision of engineering education good in Britain but employer attitudes resistant to it (Robertson, 1981). There was the suspicion that college graduates would be too superior. British employers regarded United States engineering education as including too many non-technical subjects and German education too theoretical. Accordingly while the United States fostered higher technical education on a large scale, British employers had a less sincere belief in higher education and preferred apprenticeship, on the job and evening class training.

The trade unions too were less than enthusiastic about technical education. They suspected it as something from which employers stood to gain at their expense. In particular they feared that technical colleges would overproduce skilled men and drive down their wage differentials undermining the labour aristocracy. Moreover the colleges, if they became too powerful, could undermine apprenticeship which apart from its training function was also a means by which skilled men who had served time could control the entry of their successors into the trade. The Plumbers' Union and the City and Guilds engaged in a long dispute between 1885 and 1903 as the former sought to enforce a closed shop which they suspected the latter, with its technical examinations for Plumbers, of undermining (Foden, 1970). The Bricklayers' Society was also very hostile to the teaching of bricklaying in technical colleges (Dearle, 1914). Unions, as Socialists, also disliked Junior Technical Schools, partly for the same reasons that they mistrusted technical colleges but also because they feared that such schools would direct working-class children into manual working-class jobs denying them the general education that might enable them to rise to 'white collar'.

A root problem of our supposed deficiencies in education for industry was seen to be the government's inadequate financial support for it. We have seen the low figures compared with those of Germany. Behind these lay a British concern to keep taxation and public expenditure generally low. Magnus thought that 'the fear of helping some industries at the expense of others appears to have been one of the reasons which prevented the Treasury from making grants for distinctly technological instruction' (Magnus, 1910 p. 269). Also the Victorians could pride themselves that so much was done by private initiative and philanthropy which could have been stifled by state money. Roderick and Stephens have shown the remarkable developments in Liverpool in the later nineteenth century where higher scientific education was catered for by a range of public institutions created by private money. There was the Queen's College 1857 which gave way to the University College in 1881, the School of Technical Chemistry from the 1870s to 1890s, the Liverpool College of Chemistry from 1850 to about 1910, the Liverpool School of Science of 1861 subsequently the Liverpool Polytechnic and John Moores University. Roderick and Stephens note that training for leading chemists in this region was 'largely in private hands'. The virtue of such institutions was that they arose in response to demand, were often formed by chemists and manufacturers and relied for their existence on providing a relevant service. Yet lest this be thought a strong argument for private finance rather than a criticism of the lack of state support we should consider what happened to most of these institutions. The disadvantages of the lack of state underpinning were seen in the constantly shaky finances (of Queen's and the School of Science), the low output of students (of Queen's and the College of Chemistry) and the ultimate petering out (of Queen's, the School of Technical Chemistry, the College of Chemistry). It is significant that the only survivors were what became respectively the University and the technical college, both receiving, under different auspices, state money from 1889 (Roderick and Stephens, 1972).

One fundamental reason lay behind many of the others inhibiting or delaying Britain's development of technical and scientific education for industry, namely the excessive reverence for 'liberal education'. Many scholars find this view attractive, that Britain was too much in thrall to ideals of education which predated her industrialisation and were especially associated with pre-industrial élites (Wiener, 1981, Barnett 1986, Wooldridge, 1990). Liberal education was by definition the education of a free or liberal man who had no need to seek employment or use his education for vocational purposes. It was based on the psychological belief that a mind should be developed by grappling with difficult, abstract and seemingly useless subjects – pure mathematics at Cambridge, classics at Oxford, philosophy in the Scottish universities. The 'liberality' did not imply breadth of education since in England at least deep focusing on one or two subjects was thought to be the only way to secure the rigour and discipline required. A mind so honed was a good in itself, just as was a healthy body and being physically fit, and did not need to be justified in terms of future utility. Though it was also believed that for those who needed to do so, the well-trained mind could turn itself flexibly to almost any matter. In practice this liberal education did begin to be applied to certain careers, to the Church and then to the civil service whose selection procedures from the 1850s enshrined the belief that the generally trained intelligence rather than the acquisition of specialist vocational knowledge was what was needed for the government of state and Empire. Accordingly vocational education for learning skills for jobs was regarded as inferior to the liberal training of the mind. Indeed it was particularly unfortunate in England that vocational education became associated with schools for delinquent children from the 1850s since 'industrial schools' were for the reform of young criminals rather than the industrial training of a skilled labour force. At the other extreme liberal education, by its very uselessness, its association with the ancient authorities of the classical world in literature, philosophy and mathematics, and its patrician morality, made it an appropriate education for a gentleman and a landed gentleman at that.

There was a good deal of humbug about this and psychologists in the 1930s showed that there was no especial connection between the capacity to learn one hard subject and the ability to learn another with facility as a consequence (Wooldridge, 1994). But the dangers to the education system and its relevance for industry in Victorian times and long after were twofold. It associated high prestige and high social class education with 'uselessness' and non-vocational study devoted to the higher culture of the mind. It consequently associated vocational, technical even scientific education with lower social classes, with mechanics, artisans, the working class and the dirty hands of toil. The strength of the class system and its attendant snobberies reinforced the prejudice against vocational training while engineers even today seem to feel this sense of grievance. Secondly, as the uselessness of classics, pure mathematics and philosophy had been justified in late Victorian times, so this seemed to give the justification for the proliferation of other non-vocational and 'useless' subjects in the twentieth century on the same 'liberal' grounds. Advocates of this view would see its lingering influence in the expansion of higher education after the 1960s.

3
The counterarguments

The view that defects of education held back the economy before 1914 largely held the field through the historiography of the 1960s to 1980s as it had done in most contemporary comment from the 1860s. Yet in recent years many arguments have been advanced questioning this standpoint.

First it can be argued that the British system of education was so transformed between 1870 and 1914 and especially between 1890 and 1914 that it had become an impressive support for industry rather than a liability. Following the shock of the Paris Exhibition of 1867 the system developed in various ways. A number of colleges were started in industrial provincial cities which were to grow into civic universities (Sanderson, 1972). The virtual reform of Owens College Manchester in 1873, moving to its present site in Oxford Road with substantial industrial backing began the trend. This was followed by the Yorkshire College of Science (1874) which was founded as a direct response to the Paris Exibition, then Firth College Sheffield (1879), Mason College Birmingham(1880), Liverpool University College (1881), and before 1914 they were joined by lesser colleges in South-ampton (1862), Exeter (1865), Newcastle (1871), Bristol (1876) Nottingham(1881) and Reading(1893). All these institutions were created and funded with money from local industrialists often on a substantial scale. By the mid 1900s Manchester, Liverpool, Birmingham and Leeds all had fixed capitals of around £300,000 to £400,000 and endowment incomes of £8,000 to £23,000 a year. Secondly the curricula and research of the civic universities were closely related to national and regional needs. The creation or development of bearing lubrication, colliery pumps, vanadium steel, chrome leather, gas fires, beer, soap, the quadruple expansion engine, marine radio and much else all benefited from the work of civic university researchers. Moreover a high proportion of students came from industrial and business backgrounds and about a third to a half of all students from Birmingham, Newcastle and Bristol Universities and chemists from Manchester University took up careers in industry. Students at universities rose from 5,530 in 1871 to 26,432 by 1911 and students in science and technology graduating annually in the civic universities rose from 19 in 1870 to 1,231 by 1910 while their cumulative stock rose accordingly from 127 in 1870 to 14,300 by 1910 (Roderick and Stephens, 1974).

A lower level of technical education was begun in London with the creation of Quintin Hogg's Polytechnics. These provided classes for London artisans and clerks in a whole range of technical subjects and provided an active sporting life. Starting with Regent Street in 1882 these increased in number in the 1890s to 11 by 1898. In the 1900s they moved into degree work with the result that 500 students were studying for London University degrees in 1904. Also in London, the City and Guilds of London were formed in 1879. Finsbury Technical College was set up in 1883 followed by a large Central Technical College in South Kensington in 1884. These colleges also ran a national system of technical examinations. The massive increase in this examining from 151 passes in 1879 to 14,750 by 1914 is an important indicator of the growth of technical education in these years (Millis, 1925 p. 61).

The growth of examining is explained by the development of municipal technical colleges in the 1890s following the Technical Instruction Act of 1889. This act allowed the new County Councils and County Borough Councils to levy a rate to build colleges and after 1890 the annual windfall of 'whisky money' helped to run them. Some 160 colleges were created in this way by 1898, providing much of their instruction in evening-class work. The colleges in turn spawned Junior Technical Schools – full-time technical education at school level for school children aged thirteen plus. By 1913 there were 37 such schools with 2,900 pupils, a basis for the future (Sanderson, 1994).

It is often overlooked that there was a great deal of technical education in niche areas. There were technical classes in elementary schools encouraged by code changes in 1893–6 allowing science, woodwork and metalwork. Such departments increased from 173 in 1891 to 1,396 by 1895 and by 1904 all training colleges had science departments. Secondly there were Organised Science schools supported by the Science and Art Department for work going beyond elementary work covered by the Codes. These grew from 600 students in 1860 to 187,000 by 1890. There were also older teenagers going to evening classes in technical colleges rising from 120,000 in 1893 to 474,000 by 1900 to 708,000 by 1911. Sidney Pollard is unusual in giving due recognition to these areas and finds 'the rate of expansion was truly breathtaking' (Pollard, 1989 pp. 180–1, 193–4). Also, it is usually supposed that the Mechanics Institutes of the early nineteenth century had ceased to have any serious scientific function for the artisan classes by the mid and late century (Wrigley, 1982). Yet in the North West a network of mechanics institutes formed the Union of Lancashire and Cheshire Institutes in 1872 providing library and teaching facilities for the City and Guilds and Science and Art Department examinations. One Sharp Thornber studied at Burnley Mechanics Institute between the ages of twelve and seventeen from 1870, learning enough on the technical and financial sides to set himself up as a successful cotton manufacturer (Thistlethwaite, 1996). Finally, many firms ran their own educational classes – fourteen railway companies, Brunner, Mond, United Alkali, Lever, Cadbury, Reckitts and several others (Fitzgerald, 1993).

The 1890s and 1900s were also distinctive in that they saw a positive attempt to follow the best features of the French and German systems to ensure that those nations did not continue to enjoy competitive educational advantages. The civic universities matched the German Technical High Schools and the reform by Louis Liard of the universities in France in 1896. Imperial College (1907) was intended to be the 'London Charlottenburg' to match the great TH in Berlin, just as the London School of Economics imitated the Parisian *grandes écoles* for law and politics. The stratification of secondary education in England in the 1900s deliberately imitated in simplified form the German *Gymnasium–Realschule* division and the JTS part of it was a replication of the German *Fortbildungschulen* and the French *écoles primaires supér-*

ieures (Sanderson, 1994). On the other hand Britain never understood the concept of the *Ecole Polytechnique*, a layer of higher education based on science, technology and engineering superior to the universities and educating an élite for business, politics and the military. The London polytechnics, while borrowing the name, had no such high pretensions. Also Peter Hennock has shown that we did not accept the Germanic system of dividing off engineering education into THs separate from the universities (Hennock, 1990). At the other end, Britain's wide dispersal of municipal technical colleges was probably superior in dealing with lower levels than the German and French systems, arguably reflecting the importance of the apprentice-college link in England. By 1914 it was not evident that there were serious gaps in English education compared with our major competitors that would have placed us at a disadvantage, so assiduously did we imitate and replicate.

This acceleration of activity is evident from some statistical trends. If we take six indicators of expansion across universities, technical colleges, the City and Guilds and the production of engineers we find steady growth from 1870 to 1890, becoming very rapid from 1890 to 1914. This was the 'astonishing and accelerating rate of growth' referred to by Pollard (Pollard, 1989 p. 194) and contrasts with the 'improvement came slowly' view of David Landes (Landes, 1969 p. 344).

It is plain that it is misleading to consider 1870 to 1914 as one period, as economic historians have tended to do. Before 1890 English education was defective, lacking a proper structure of universities, state and local government finance, technical colleges, free and compulsory elementary education or popular secondary education. 1870–90 was the dangerous period when we risked falling behind and it was the last phase when we had modestly good growth rates (1.2 per cent GDP per man year) compared with our competitors, yet with a poor educational system. After 1890, however, the situation was transformed with free and compulsory elementary education, the restructuring of the secondary system and the creation of a scholarship ladder in the 1900s, the elevation of civic university colleges into independent degree granting institutions with state grants from 1889, the spread of the polytechnics, municipal technical colleges and City and Guilds examinations that need no reiteration. Whereas an

Table 3.1

	(a) Univ. students	(b) Students graduating in sc. and tech. in civic univs.	(c) Cum. stock of (b)	(d) C and G passes	(e) Students in tech. college evening classes	(f) Day students in engineering classes in 4 colleges	(g) Royal Society of Arts Examination Candidates	Papers sat
1870	5530	19	127			114		
1879				151				
1880	10573	55	512	515		119		
1890	16013	166	1447	3507		193	2315	
1893					120000			
1900	17839	378	4984	8114	475000	376	9000	9808
1910	26432	1231	14300	14105		613		
1911					708000			30000
1914				14570				

(a) Lowe (1983).
(b) Roderick and Stephens (1974).
(c) Roderick and Stephens (1974).
(d) Millis (1925), p. 61.
(e) Pollard (1989), p. 179.
(f) Guagnini (1993), p. 33.
(g) Hudson and Luckhurst (London, 1954).

Englishman of 1950 would scarcely recognise the education system of 1880, that of 1910 would be quite familiar. Nor would it be unfamiliar to a Frenchman or German of 1910 who would recognise many parallel characteristics.

Why did the situation change so sharply after 1890 rather than 1870? Several factors lie behind this timing. Twenty years of government investigations into education and the economy (Samuelson 1868, Devonshire 1871–5, Samuelson 1884) had culminated in the Royal Commission on the Great Depression in 1886 with yet another volume on education, followed by Lord Selbourne's Commission on the University of London in 1889. Between 1868 and 1889 there was scarcely a year without some government investigation taking evidence, reporting on or publicising the issue which had become supersaturated in the public mind. Also 1889 was the year of the most spectacular Paris exhibition hitherto, with the new Eiffel Tower as its showpiece, yet again making England defensive about the public competitive display of its manufactures. Moreover the German patent act of 1876 encouraged the rapid growth of German research laboratories and employment of graduates in the 1880s. It was manifest in the near trebling of German dye exports in the 1880s and the 'Made in Germany' and 'Charlottenburgitis' scares of the 1890s. The 1880s were also the decade when Britain began to lose its world predominance, overtaken by the United States in GDP per man year around 1880 and in the virility symbol of steel production by the United States in the 1880s and by Germany in the 1890s. All these factors focused around 1890 rather than around 1870 as the turning point for more urgent action.

Historians have believed that defects in education were a cause of economic retardation because Victorians believed and reiterated it. Yet this view was propagated by a lobby of notable figures linked by personal friendship and often through the National Association for the Promotion of Technical Education founded in 1887 and which acted as a unifying organisation. If we take twenty leading names in the field we find that thirteen of these were academics or academic administrators, twelve were politicians in Parliament or local government often with overlapping careers.[1]

[1] The sample is Lyon Playfair, Philip Magnus, T. H. Huxley, Henry Roscoe,

Only six were industrialists and it lent weight to the suspicion that the technical education issue was one driven much more by academics and politicians out to advance careers or find a cause rather than businessmen seeking a profit. Sidney Pollard observed, 'the agitation was clearly self interested; it came from a lobby of scientists who wanted more status and more resources, and must on that account be suspect' (Pollard, 1989 p. 122). John Burns was more tart, he dismissed the 'rage for technical education' as an enthusiasm of 'well intentioned philanthropic persons (who) had nothing better to do' (Saint, 1989 p. 75). Economists of the time always tended to stress education as the cure for Britain's economic ills whereas businessmen did not believe they suffered from a lack of training. Sir William Armstrong refuting the 'vague cry for technical education' saw the factory not the college as the place for training workmen. Neither side had any empirical evidence for one view or the other and for the historian it is as reasonable to accept the views of a very successful technological industrialist like Armstrong as those of professors and politicians with axes to grind (Evans and Wiseman, 1984).

Next, historians are taking a more positive view of apprentice-ship than Edwardian writers did. It was an assumption of critics of the English system that apprenticeship was declining – the 'decline of apprenticeship' was a familiar phrase of the 1900s. Usually such critics called for more college and school education in technology and crafts to substitute for this decline. The further assumption was that our relative lack of college training, compared with Continental systems, was an indication of backwardness. Yet on the contrary, it is now being appreciated that apprenticeship was preferred in England on rational grounds. It placed the costs of training on the employer who initially paid more than an appren-tice was worth and whose training was a cost. The apprentice also paid in accepting lower wages in his early apprenticeship than he might have gained as a labourer and in his later apprenticeship than his work was probably worth. The assumption was that both would recoup themselves later – the employer through high value

Lord Haldane, Bernhard Samuelson, A. J. Mundella, Quintin Hogg, Norman Lockyer, Arthur Acland, Swire Smith, William Garnett, Sidney Webb, Michael Sadler, John Donnelly, Matthew Arnold, John Slagg, Frederick Mappin, H. Llewellyn Smith, William Armstrong (who had changed his position).

work and a skilled labour force and the craftsman in higher differentials of wages. The cost of training was accordingly born by the ultimate beneficiaries, the employer and employed through initally foregone and then recouped wages and profits. On balance apprenticeship training was probably at the expense of the men, the apprentices themselves and their mentors. It was one reason why some employers favoured trade unions as the defenders of the apprenticeship system. This contrasted with Continental assumptions of publicly funded college education where the cost was borne by tax and rate payer. The English apprenticeship arrangements were quite as logical and arguably more equitable than college based ones – different but not inferior, and systems were not to be judged by the numbers of students in formal college places (Nicholas, 1985). The same issue now arises over who should bear the cost of university education, the student beneficiary or the tax payer?

If the rationale of apprenticeship is now being rejustified so is the practice. Keith McClelland, considering engineering and shipbuilding, finds that in spite of dilution vast numbers of craftsmen were needed to set tools and maintain machinery as well as to engage in production. He concludes, 'in the end a shop floor practical training in which apprenticeship remained of central importance continued to be the most favoured means of transmitting skills in the engineering and shipbuilding industries' (McClelland, 1990). Bernard Elbaum also finds that what is remarkable about apprenticeship in Britain before 1914 is not its decline but its survival; it verified worthiness, was cheap and led to stability of employment (Elbaum, 1991). Apprenticeship was not only important for the working class but for upper-class entrants to engineering who served as premium paying apprentices in the offices of leading engineers whether university graduates or not (Guagnini, 1993). In areas like shipbuilding and engineering it delivered the goods effectively. Roderick Floud has shown just how apprentice based engineering education was. Of the 126 members of the Institution of Mechanical Engineers who died in 1890, 1900, 1910 and 1920 (presumably having most of their careers in the period between 1870 and 1914) 119 (94.4 per cent) had served an apprenticeship and only 24 (19 per cent) had had any higher education. Yet Floud finds training 'well attuned to the economic environment of the time' and 'the British system was able to supply skilled engineers to man the industry both at home and abroad' (Floud, 1982).

We have seen that part of the belief in the inadequacies of English education for industry was linked with an admiration for the supposed superiority of German education in this regard. Yet this viewpoint has come under increasing criticism. The *Volksschule* has been demystified, 'it is a fable that Prussia has the best elementary schools in the world', its teachers were poorly paid and their schools left the German people 'culturally divided and unprepared for the trials of the twentieth century' (Anderson, 1970). It secured for Prussia 99 per cent male and 98 per cent female literacy by 1898 but this was not notably greater than that of Britain. Pollard has also shown that the literacy of German emigrants to the United States was lower than that of Englishmen (Pollard, 1989 p. 147). At the secondary school level the *Gymnasium* was quite as focused on classical studies as were the English public schools and this was the most common form of schooling for German businessmen (59.2 per cent) (Berghoff and Moller, 1994), not the more practical *Realschule*. At the higher education level too there were misconceptions. German universities over-produced theologians, philosophers and lawyers and their gradu-ates aspired to the civil service quite as much as any Oxbridge high flyer. As regards German university science although its organic chemistry was undoubtedly superior yet this was not evidently so for mathematics and physics, engineering or metallurgy. Also there was a surprising parity in that 29.7 per cent of English businessmen born after 1860 and active by 1914 had been to university; the same figure for Germany was only 30.6 per cent (Berghoff and Moller, 1994). We are also reminded that the THs, so revered in England, did not have the prestige of universities. Only in 1899 were the THs allowed to award doctorates, giving them equivalence with universities, and even then 'the sense of inferiority remained' (James, 1990). This had the unfortunate effect that teachers at THs increasingly neglected the applied sciences in pursuit of theoretical science appropriate for 'proper' universities. In any case about 40 per cent of the students at THs came from the *Gymnasien* (50 per cent in the universities), not from technically oriented schools. The proportion of intake to both universities and THs from *Realgymnasien* and *Oberrealschulen* was remarkably similar also at just over 20 per cent (Lundgreen, 1984). The trend of recent writing has been to modify the views of contemporary historians based on Victorian views that the Germans had an education system at all levels geared to superior literacy and the output of scientists and technicians. It had much more in common with the English system in its reverence for classical and academic traditions, social selectivity and the production of the scholar and professional man. Lundgreen estimating the contribution of the education of the labour force to German economic growth in the nineteenth century attributes only 'a meagre contribution of a bare 2 per cent' (Lundgreen, 1975). In any case it was easily forgotten that it was only after 1950 and certainly not before 1914 that Germany surpassed the United Kingdom in GDP per head. Pollard is scathing on the pre 1914 period 'altogether it would be hard to maintain that Germany derived much gain and much in the way of superiority over Britain' (Pollard, 1989 p. 162).

Floud urges us to regard British education not as inferior to that of competitor nations but as one rational option within a spectrum. At one end was the German system with a state supported range of industrial education from kindergarten to trade and technical schools. At the other end was the United States with virtually no industrial schools receiving government aid but with an emphasis on training by employers. In the middle was the British system with the employer providing training in the detailed practice of the trade but not the theoretical background which would enable the worker to rise to positions of greater responsibility. It was assumed that this would be gained by voluntary part-time attendance at a technical college. Both the British and French systems provided extensive part-time technical education which encouraged the social mobility of workers but which was lacking in the American and German systems. Floud argues that the British system whereby employees voluntarily sought to improve their value by choosing extra general training in college is more rational. It was an appropriate free market solution to the creation of human capital and not a cause of Britain's long-term decline (Floud, 1984).

Next it can be argued that to Victorians it would not be evident that there was any obvious connection between the success and failure of certain industries and the education behind them. The failure of the dyestuffs industry and the lack of organic chemistry is the clearest case and those who wish to stress the connection lay much emphasis on it (Wrigley, 1986). Yet if we consider a range of successful and less successful industries the relevance of education becomes quite unclear.

Shipbuilding was the British industry most secure from foreign competition. Britain made 50–60 per cent of world tonnage, we had the largest navy and merchant marine in the world and the only shipbuilding industry large enough to be efficient. The major technical advances, the compound engines and turbines, were British and productivity and real wages rose steadily. Yet Paul Robertson denies the relevance of education for this (Robertson, 1974). Entrepreneurs preferred on the job training to technical education. They neglected the new university departments at Glasgow, Newcastle and Liverpool and only one fifth of apprentices in the North East took any technical college evening class examinations. Britain's competitors on the other hand paid far more attention to technical education but in Robertson's view it did not pay off for them and Britain was right not to invest more in technical education for this industry. Metallurgical mining provided a converse case. This was a very successful industry which had good educational support but not enough of it. British firms would have been eager to employ more British mining and metallurgical graduates had they been available. Yet this did not hold back the industry, 'investment in mining and metallurgical education may have been quite limited before 1914, but this did not significantly frustrate the activities of those intent on grabbing a big share of the world metal mining industry' (Harvey and Press, 1989). The cotton industry was by far Britain's chief export and remained so until the late 1930s and historians have shown that its technology was appropriate and not backward. Yet this was an industry with very little educational back up. Even Manchester University, which was supported by the industry, had no cotton textile department since workers were trained on the job from the ages of twelve or thirteen. This range of successful industries accordingly presents a curious spectrum in their relations with education – one had good education which was neglected, one good education which was insufficient and the third scarcely any at all.

If we turn to some industries of questionable success then we find similar disjunctions. Scarcely any industry other than dye-stuffs aroused such feelings of guilt as steel. We were overtaken in steel production by the United States in the 1880s and by Germany in the 1890s and a host of reasons have been advanced for this including inevitably education (Musgrave, 1967). Yet this was an industry very well served in metallurgical education by Sheffield University which was well used and appreciated by local firms and admired by the Germans (Sanderson, 1978; Eason, 1996). Yet Temin has suggested that such were the global problems of the British steel industry in terms of location of raw materials and markets that its educational support whether good or bad could have made virtually no difference to its fortunes (Temin, 1966). McCloskey takes another tack, finding the British steel industry's performance good up to 1900 but diminishing in the 1900–14 period, precisely when metallurgical education was most effective (McCloskey, 1973). So both Temin and McCloskey, contrary to Musgrave, would find education quite marginal to steel's problems. At the local level education has been found to be irrelevant to the success or failure of the Teeside steel industry at this time (Le Guillon, 1981). Coal is rather similar but the converse. This was an industry with good output, profits and exports though it was criticised for its poor productivity and technical change. Yet at the managerial level this was one of the best educated industries of all since it was the only one where managers were obliged to be qualified (by Acts of 1887 and 1903) and many excellent university and college departments (Birmingham, Newcastle, Leeds, Cardiff, Wigan and others) provided these courses and qualifications. It was thus an unusual industry with a considerable gap between well-educated managers and an ill-educated labour force producing and exporting successfully in bulk if rather inefficiently (Church, 1986). Accordingly the experience of troubled industries was as varied as the successful, both steel and coal paradoxically being well served with education which did little to offset their problems in other directions. Thus a Victorian could be forgiven for not readily seeing any convincing connection between education and the fortunes of some of his chief industries.

Some writers would go further. The concern about education

was linked with the belief not only in the superiority of the Germans but that British entrepreneurs were performing badly, and this was the tone of much writing of the 1960s (Aldcroft, 1964). However, not only is there not much evident connection between education and the economic success or failure of certain industries as we have suggested, the overall problem of 'failure' is now regarded as having been exaggerated. Revisionism in a range of studies dealing with cotton, steel, coal, machine tools has found that rates of technical change and productivity compared well with the competition. So if the problem does not exist then education can hardly be blamed for creating it. As Stephen Nicholas suggests, 'recent work on British growth and productivity found little evidence that the economy experienced failure. As a result the deficiencies in technical and scientific education, if they existed, are a cause without an effect.' (Nicholas, 1985).

In Scotland too, recent literature has been tilting towards a more revisionist optimistic position. It has been argued that the Scottish universities were much behind the English civic universities in relating themselves to industry (Sanderson, 1972 chapter 6). Except in engineering the universities developed little of use to business and industry. Scottish businessmen showed less interest in their universities than the English did in theirs and this reflected itself in an unwillingness to employ graduates or support their institutions financially. However Paul Robertson has made a spirited defence of Scottish universities. He agrees that the universities were weak in training graduates for scientific and commercial careers for most of the nineteenth century but points to the sharp increase in the proportions of students at Glasgow and Edinburgh studying science and engineering at the turn of the century. At Edinburgh the number of undergraduates studying engineering annually rose from 3 or 4 percent in the 1890s to 26 per cent by 1910–14. The similar figures for Glasgow were a rise from 9 or 10 per cent in the 1890s to 59 per cent by 1910–14. In the four Scottish universities, by 1914, 54 per cent of graduates became scientists and engineers compared with 16.5 per cent teachers and 8 per cent doctors. Robertson reminds us that Glasgow and Edinburgh were not like the small English civic universities – they were much larger; Glasgow at 2,916 students was nearly three times as large as Manchester, which was the largest English civic university, having 1,014 students in 1913. Accordingly Glasgow and Edinburgh were 'two of the most important institutions for training British engineers and scientists in the years before 1914' (Robertson, 1984). Moreover, focusing on Glasgow, Robertson finds that a third to a half of its students came from higher industrial and commercial families: 'Glasgow's position as a university catering to the children of industrial and commercial families was quite distinct' (Robertson, 1990). But Robertson concedes that far fewer went back into industrial jobs – 13.9 per cent at the peak in 1913 compared with 20.9 per cent who went into medicine and 34.9 per cent into teaching. In sum, Robertson finds a closer engagement between Scottish universities and industry than had been thought in terms of the social background of parents, the size of their output of scientists and engineers and their sharp increase in student numbers in the 1890s. This is in accordance with the optimistic view, though the lack of interest of business employers for most of the nineteenth century and the channelling of sons of business families into the professions were still evidence of a distancing between Scottish universities and business and industry.

Finally, for Britain as a whole, the most detailed work on economic growth finds a positive connection between education and economic growth for this period. Matthews, Feinstein and Odling Smee find that the growth of labour quality resulting from improvements in education, annual percentage growth rates rose from 0.3 per cent in the period from 1856–1873 to 0.5 per cent in the period 1873–1913 and remained at 0.5 per cent or 0.6 per cent thereafter until 1973 (Mathews, Feinstein and Odling Smee, 1982). They also see education as the most important source of the improvement of labour quality. So the period from 1873 to 1913 is not one where education began to fail the economy; on the contrary it was one where modern levels of contribution were achieved for the first time.

In all these ways doubt is being thrown upon the assumptions of Victorians and subsequent historians about defects of education of the labour force as underlying the fact that the British economy fell behind before 1914. But we should turn to consider whether these defects are more justly attributable to the education of a higher social class.

4
The education of the élite, 1870–1914

The education provided by the public schools and Oxford and Cambridge had long been that enjoyed by the élite, usually landed, ruling classes of Britain. During the Industrial Revolution a parallel élite emerged of industrial and commercial wealth. These were often excluded from the public schools and ancient universities by their nonconformity until such discrimination was removed in the 1850s and by the Universities' Tests Act of 1871. From the 1870s landed, ruling, professional and business élites, on the basis of their wealth from disparate origins, could share a more common school and university education. How far these schools and universities became more open to a wider élite will be examined later. This mattered because their education shaped not only the attitudes of policy makers but the types and levels of expertise brought by industrialists to their businesses and their own notions of what was adequate and appropriate for their needs.

The public schools have come in for much criticism as peculiar institutions inimical to business and industry. They have been accused of transmitting the values of the 'Christian gentleman', as Thomas Arnold put it, emphasising the acceptance of privilege in return for responsibilities and seeing careers in the public service, Church and professions as the best expressions of such values. Leisure was seen as worth cultivating for its own sake by gentlemen amateurs while games playing brought out co-operative team playing rather than individual endeavour. The public schools, especially the more ancient, stressed the importance of historic communities, the subordination of the individual to the community, deference to social rank and acceptance of tradition. Above all, in the present context they held a low view of trade.

Trade required private enterprise and innovation rather than conservative tradition and sacrifice to public service: 'individualist, grasping and eminently rational the entrepreneur was diametrically opposed to the public school ethos' (Wilkinson, 1964 p. 18). Moreover the public schools gave pride of place to the classics and the belief that such studies provided a general 'liberal education' in reasoning and memory. But in doing so they placed a lower value on stimulating the creative imagination and a lower one still on science and technological studies as too specialised, narrowly utilitarian and irrelevant to future public schoolboy careers. Wilkinson claims, 'public school life militated against entrepreneur qualities – creative imagination, friendliness to innovation' (Wilkinson 1964) and following Wilkinson, Wiener (1981) and Barnett (1986) have seen the public schools as major villains in Britain's industrial decline.

Although there may be a broad truth in these findings there have been several differently shaded interpretations of the relationship of the public schools to the economy. First there is the optimistic view that the public schools underwent significant change from about the 1860s and adjusted to industrial society successfully. Whereas it is fair to say that the public schools neglected science in the first half of the nineteenth century many took it up with enthusiasm in the second half. Various reasons lay behind this. The Clarendon Commission report on the public schools (1864) urged them to teach science and the evidence of J. M. Winter, the pioneering science master at Rugby provided an exemplar. The reception of the Clarendon Report coincided with the Paris Exhibition of 1867 and the Samuelson Select Committee of 1868 and Matthew Arnold's Report on Prussian education also in 1868. The concern about public schools was thus drawn into the wider concern about education, science and industrial competitiveness. Moreover the entrance examinations of the Royal Military Academy at Sandhurst required two science subjects from the mid 1850s. The victories of the Prussian army in the 1860s had made plain the importance of artillery and gave urgency to raising the educational level of British officers after the Crimean War. Whereas the teaching of science in the public schools had been held back by the lack of suitable teachers in the early nineteenth century, the new Natural Sciences Tripos at

Cambridge (1848) and the Honours School of Natural Science at Oxford (1852) now provided science graduates from the ancient universities who were gentlemen and Anglican and hence suitable as public school masters and who could in turn prepare boys for the new science degrees at Oxford and Cambridge. Changes at Oxford and Cambridge broke the log jam which had prevented the public schools from espousing science earlier. Accordingly J. M. Winter started science teaching at Rugby in 1859 and it became compulsory from 1864. Harrow also began from 1859, Clifton from 1862 and Winchester from 1866 while Wellington began its 'modern' side for army entrants in the 1860s. Some schools built notable laboratories, Oundle in the 1890s, Westminster in 1903 and Rugby, which already had a pioneering laboratory from the 1860s also built a new one in 1903. This echoed the spate of industrial and university research laboratory building before 1914.

If the curriculum changed, so did the value systems of the schools. The Arnoldian ideal of the early decades of the century had been that of the 'Christian gentleman', the academic scholarly boy much exercised with his religious conscience. These were schoolmasters, clergymen and dons in the making – much like Arnold himself – but hardly entrepreneurs and managers. More secular values were introduced to the schools in the 1860s by the encouragement of games and athleticism (Mangan, 1981). Rules were codified to facilitate inter-school competition. Thus new schools, of which there was a new wave of building in the 1860s, were surrounded by ample playing fields which impressed parents and emphasised the importance of games. The games playing made boys fit, of virile physique, developed qualities of character, self confidence and leadership, encouraged sociability and team working to achieve goals and discouraged bookishness – all qualities attractive to business and industry. Alongside the sports came the military corps, growing out of the Volunteers and rifle clubs (Best, 1975). In any case young gentlemen owned guns and shot for sport while schools employed ex-sergeant majors to teach physical training and drill. Corps formalised in the 1860s with fears of potential war with Napoleon III, received a further stimulus with the Boer War and crystallised as the Officers' Training Corps with the Haldane army reforms in 1908. These inculcated the same secular values as games playing but added an even greater concern for authority, control and order. The secularisation of the ethos was matched by a laicisation of staff. In 1870 54 per cent of the staff of ten leading public schools were clergymen but by 1906 this number had fallen to 13.6 per cent (Honey, 1977). This change of ethos from godliness to manliness, secular values and qualities of character made ex-public school boys more attractive to the business world than the Arnoldian gentleman.

As the public schools became more attractive in curriculum and ethos so there was a sharp increase in the number of sons of businessmen attending public schools. At Winchester the percentage of boys' fathers in business and industry rose; the proportion who were sons of businessmen rose from small single figures in the early part of the century to consistently a quarter by the 1880s and thereafter. Another reason for the increasing proportion of businessmen was that they could afford the rising costs. In the 1850s many of the leading public schools started entrance examinations. This had several effects. It gave rise to a sector of preparatory schools to prepare for entrance, these rose from 20 in 1850 to 400 by 1900 and by 1890 Harrow was fed by 134 different preparatory schools (Honey, 1977). This probably raised the intellectual level of the public schools but by increasing the overall expense of a preparatory plus public school education an advantage was given to those of a wealthy background.

In turn increasing proportions of public schoolboys themselves chose careers in business and industry before 1914. Whereas negligible proportions of public schoolboys had taken up such careers in the early nineteenth century, from the 1890s fairly consistent proportions of between 25 and 35 per cent were doing so across a wide range of schools studied by different historians. See table 4.1.

This is also reflected in the increasing proportion of company directors who were ex-public schoolboys over this time (Stanworth, 1980).

		1860–79	1880–99	1900–19
Total public schools	industry	58.3	62.3	72.6
	finance	75.9	76.3	78.1
Total Clarendon schools	industry	35.7	33.4	35.5
	finance	46.5	50.7	46.5

Table 4.1 Percentage of public schoolboys choosing careers in business and industry

	1860s	1870s	1880s	1890s	1900s	1910s
Winchester[a]	24	29	33	35	37	33
Clifton[b]	9		16		25	
Marlborough[b]	17		23		23	
Merchant Taylors[b]		13		42		25
Mill Hill[b]		31		30	32	
Harrow and Rugby[c]		6.9		20.7		
St Oswalds, Ellesmere[d]				21		
Loretto[e]				36		
Sedburgh[e]		30		30		

(a) Bishop and Wilkinson (1967) pp. 64–9.
(b) Reader (1966) Appendix 2 'Public Schoolboys Occupations 1807–1911'.
(c) Bamford (1967).
(d) Heward (1988), p. 140.
(e) Ward (1967).

The trend is most marked for the newer Victorian public schools. This also makes the point that public school boys were more influential in finance than in manufacturing industry. Changes in public school curriculum and ethos stimulated increases in the number of boys coming from business and industrial backgrounds and going back to such careers. Yet there are fine shades of debate about the extent of the contact between the public schools and business and industry and the desirability or otherwise of it.

Firstly, there are those who are sceptical about the level of commitment of the schools to science. Colin Shrosbree reminds us that although the Clarendon Commission in 1864 recommended the promotion of science in the public schools yet the subsequent Public Schools Act in 1868 offered no guidance on the curriculum and only one of the Special Commissioners appointed to oversee its enforcement was a scientist. The Act was concerned with the finance and constitutions of the schools and there may have been hope that scientists would begin to exercise an influence through the more open boards of governors. Yet 'the Act did not in itself initiate any reform of the curriculum: the schools obtained what was virtually voluntary unspecified reform over an indefinite period. There was no immediate necessity to introduce proper science teaching and many schools did not do so for many years' (Shrosbee, 1988 p. 203). Meadows and Brock point out that in the 1870s of 128 endowed schools science was taught in only about a half (63) and of these only 13 had laboratories and only 18 any apparatus. They suggest that 'no really fundamental progress in the position of science in the public schools took place throughout the remainder of the century'. This was largely because parents did not care, since they did not see science as relevant to the future careers of their sons (Meadows and Brock, 1975). Likewise Roderick and Stephens point out that in the 1870s of over 3,000 pupils in six public schools only 6 per cent went on to study science and 4 per cent engineering (Roderick and Stephens, 1972). This may be a reflection of the fact that of all headmasters of public schools appointed between 1860 and 1960 only 1 or 2 per cent were scientists (Honey, 1987). Elizabeth Krumpe's study of the headmasters of the Clarendon schools between 1860 and 1914 shows that of the 29 only six (a fifth) came from business backgrounds. Of the group eleven followed policies which encouraged science in the curriculum in some way and only two expressed positive hostility to science. Yet Krumpe's conclusion is not quite as optimistic as her data, 'all twenty-nine headmasters agreed that the classical course of study created the truly educated man'. Later headmasters 'were forced to recognise that the times demanded men trained in science, mathematics and modern languages ... (yet) ... they made little effort to experiment in a meaningful way with the curriculum' (Krumpe, 1987 pp. 298–9).

A second pessimistic view is that public schoolboys did indeed go into business and industry but they did more harm than good there. This is the view of Bishop and Wilkinson, who showed the sharp increase in Winchester boys taking up business and industrial careers. Yet they had reservations that such boys were merely returning to their own family firms where family connections were more important than their abilities. They pose the paradox that whereas the armed forces and civil service were becoming careers open to talent, private business was becoming more nepotistic, with firms being carried on by ex-public schoolboy sons who returned to management after a school education quite lacking in relevance to their future careers. The firms were stultified thereby

(Bishop and Wilkinson, 1967 pp. 188–9). Charlotte Erickson finds a similar situation in the steel industry where public school-boys went into the industry but their lack of technical training diminished their value to it. Only 10 per cent of steelmasters in 1865, 16 per cent in the period 1875–95 and then 31 per cent in the period 1905–25 had such training. Moreover, the family connection for some stifled the career advancement of those below them who had technical expertise but lower social standing (Erickson, 1959).

A third argument is that the public schools positively diverted boys away from business and industry. D. C. Ward accuses them of causing 'a haemorrhage of talent' away from industry because the irrelevance of the public school curricula failed to prepare boys for such careers and so provide a reservoir of management and technological talent (Ward, 1967). Yet Ward was among the first to show that about a third of public schoolboys actually went into industrial careers – which was hardly a 'haemorrhage'. An interesting finesse of this argument is that the fact that businessmen sent their boys to public schools may actually have been beneficial, since it may have positively diverted them from industrial careers and cleared them from the path of thrusters from below (Coleman, 1973). This too seemed undermined by Coleman's own findings that a half of Courtaulds' directors were public school men by 1914 and 82 per cent by 1938. It is interesting that this argument that public school men did not go into industry is seen by Ward as an undesirable haemorrhage and by Coleman as a desirable clearing away. Yet curiously the statistics of both cast doubt on their arguments.

A fourth argument is that the public schools were neither good nor bad for industry but irrelevant. Berghoff suggests that we are looking through the wrong end of the telescope, that what matters is not the proportion of public schoolboys going into industry but that of businessmen who were former public schoolboys (Berghoff, 1990). In his study of Birmingham, Bristol and Manchester he finds 'that the relevance of public schools for a study of the late nineteenth-century business community has been gravely exaggerated, for only a mere 18 per cent of all entrepreneurs ... had attended one of these élite institutions ... the overall impact of these schools on the entire business class must have been very limited indeed'. This is confirmed by David Jeremy's analysis of the Dictionary of Business Biography where only 12.7 per cent of businessmen born between 1840 and 1869 (and active, say, 1860–1914) attended a leading public school or 20.6 per cent any kind of public school (Jeremy, 1984) .

The most elaborate exposition of the slight relevance of the public schools is that of W. D. Rubinstein. By use of probate records he shows that parents of public schoolboys were predominantly professional and middle class. Fewer than 4 per cent of the potential middle class attended any public school and still less an élite one in the 1860s and fewer than 7 per cent by the end of the century. The public schools were predominantly for the professional classes whose sons tended to enter the professions. Businessmen's sons likewise followed their fathers and the drift from the business to any other occupation was 'amazingly small'. Rubinstein suggests that 'the public schools simply did not produce a haemorrhage of talent away from business life ... too few sons of entrepreneurs attended a public school to make any real difference' (Rubinstein, 1993).

However, one area on which there is agreement is the importance of public school men in banking (Cassis, 1985). Public school men constituted 44 per cent of London bankers in the period 1890–1914 and even more significantly 62 per cent of those educated between 1861 and 1880. Social contacts and social ease, a sense of honour, integrity, discretion and 'good form' that a public school education sought to foster were most appropriate for this sector and the lack of scientific education was no drawback. Stanworth's figures on company directors cited above also indicated that public school boys had more impact in finance than in manufacturing and this is in accord with W. D. Rubinstein's insight that Britain has always been much more based on mercantile and financial activity than manufacturing industry.

Oxford and Cambridge, like the public schools that fed them, have both received severe criticism. Correlli Barnett has criticised the Oxbridge devotion to liberal education, the belief that the mind-training qualities of non-vocational 'useless' knowledge such as classics and pure mathematics created minds which were 'judicious, balanced and cautious rather than operational and engaged' (Barnett, 1986 p. 215). These universities neglected science and, even more, technology; they produced clergymen and civil servants rather than businessmen and indeed emasculated the sons of businessmen into gentlemen and diverted them to the professions. To the extent that this was so then the ancient universities would have been forces working against industry and the economy and contributing to the 'decline of the industrial spirit' (Wiener, 1981).

In the early nineteenth century both universities shared several characteristics which distanced them from the economy. They excluded nonconformists and hence much of the business élite of the Midlands and the North, although nonconformists could matriculate but not graduate at Cambridge. Their tutors were celibate bachelor clergymen living in college and isolated from secular careers. The curricula were narrowly focused on mathematics at Cambridge and classics at Oxford and two-thirds of Oxford and a half of Cambridge graduates became clergymen. The whole system was ossified by the self-interest of the colleges and fellows protecting their finances and autonomy against the encroachment of the central organisation of their universities. By the 1870s many of these matters had been reformed. Nonconformists were allowed to both matriculate and graduate at Oxford from 1854 and Cambridge from 1856 and become fellows following the Universities' Tests Act of 1871 which also removed the requirement for them to be ordained clergy. The prohibitions against marriage were removed by college statutes in the 1870s and 1880s. This made possible both the reception of sons of nonconformist business families and the employment of secular married dons with contacts with the worlds of business outside (Engel, 1983). The new subjects such as engineering, industrial chemistry, economics could not have developed without such men. Curricular diversification was brought about by the institution of the Natural Sciences Tripos at Cambridge and the Honours School of Natural Science at Oxford. To support these, the Oxford Museums with laboratories was built in 1860 and the Clarendon Laboratory in 1870 and the chemistry laboratories during 1877–9. At Cambridge the great Cavendish Laboratory was build in the early 1870s followed by the steady building of university science laboratories in virtually every year up to 1914. In turn these developments were reinforced by a shift of resources from rich colleges to the central university coffers. The Duke of Cleveland's Commission in 1873 showed for the first time just how wealthy the colleges were. At Oxford the annual income of the colleges in 1871 was £727,849 and that of the Cambridge colleges was £604,821 which compared with the meagre incomes of their universities – £79,738 at Oxford and £57,691 at Cambridge. The resulting Oxford and Cambridge Act of 1877 obliged the colleges to transfer some of their funds to the universities to create science professorships. The reforms seemed to have paved the way for the ancient universities to play a more relevant role in the modern world, not least in relation to the economy.

Although both Oxford and Cambridge shared the same reforms at the same time yet their fortunes sharply diverged in the 1870–1914 period. Oxford failed to develop industrially relevant science subjects though Cambridge embraced them eagerly. Why this divergence? Janet Howarth identifies various reasons for Oxford's poor performance in science (Howarth, 1987). Oxford had an active scientific culture in the early nineteenth century but became inferior to Cambridge from the 1860s. Firstly, Oxford unfortunately appointed two professors, William Odling for chemistry and R. B. Clifton for physics. Their careers had been able before coming to Oxford but flagged thereafter and, with no retirement age, they remained as dead hands over Oxford science until the First World War. Secondly, the 'Young Oxford' movement of the 1880s emphasised Oxford's role in the humanities, Church and politics and focused hostility to science as, falsely, no part of Oxford's tradition. Thirdly, Oxford was less successful than Cambridge in transferring funds from the colleges to the university. Cambridge levied taxes on the colleges and financed new appointments from a Common University Fund and by 1886 Cambridge had three times as many science lecturers as Oxford. Fourthly, Oxford took more of its students from the leading public schools where science was a low priority, as we have seen. Fifthly Oxford required scientists to continue the study of the classics to a greater extent and later than Cambridge. And finally, fundamentally, Oxford industrial science – in contrast to its medical science – never acquired entrepreneurial department builders such as abounded in Cambridge.

There was also the problem of the agricultural depression. The fall in agricultural and especially grain prices in the 1870s to 1890s hit the colleges and universities hard, since they derived a substantial part of their income from rents. Dunbabin studying Oxford and Cambridge considers the impact of the depression exaggerated since housing rents helped to offset land rents but admits that the depression was a 'check to an earlier rapid expansion' (Dunbabin, 1975). Engel, focusing on Oxford specifically, considers that Dunbabin underestimates the adverse effect on that university (Engel, 1978, 1983). The depression prevented the development of readerships and prize fellowships and the consequent financial stringency entrenched anti-scientific anti-research attitudes at Oxford. Michael Jones paints a more nuanced picture with the richer Oxford colleges becoming richer but the poor poorer with the university suffering a diminution of income from £11,708 to £9,875 between 1871 and 1893 and the contributions of the colleges to the university falling from about £8,000 to £6,000 between 1883 and 1893 (Jones, 1997). Both Engel and Jones are clear, for Oxford, that through the effect it had on damaging the possibilities for Oxford science, the agricultural depression diminished Britain's industrial competitiveness. In Jones's words 'the aspirations of the 1878–82 commissioners to encourage science there (at Oxford) through a financial restructuring remained largely unfulfilled. The agricultural depression, therefore, provided an unexpected obstacle to the modernisation of higher education in Britain.'

If Oxford and Cambridge underwent the same reforms and suffered the same agricultural depression, yet the outcomes for Cambridge were vastly different. Cambridge, in sharp contrast to Oxford, developed a range of teaching and research in subjects relevant to industry (Sanderson, 1972). In chemistry Sir James Dewar was the inventor of the Dewar's vacuum flask for storing liquid gas, quinoline for combating malaria and he was the co-inventor of cordite as well as undertaking a range of industrial research for firms including Gilbey's port and Edison's light filaments. James Stuart started engineering in 1875 as the first professor building up laboratory practice and his successor Sir Alfred Ewing began the Mechanical Sciences Tripos in 1894 and by 1903 over 8 per cent of Cambridge undergraduates were studying engineering (Hilken, 1967). This was in sharp contrast with Oxford which did not begin engineering until 1907 – probably the last world-class university to do so – but with no laboratory until 1914. Cambridge became probably the leading university in the world for physics, initially closely related to electrical engineering with the work of Clerk Maxwell 1873–9 and Lord Rayleigh 1879–84. Its greatest achievements however were associated with the work in nuclear physics of J. J. Thompson the discoverer of the electron. Even mathematics, formerly criticised for its excessive purity in the 1850s was highly practical in the late nineteenth century with the Lucasian professor Sir George Stokes being a notable civil engineer on bridges, harbour and sea canal work. Outside the sciences Alfred Marshall 1885–1908 developed the economics of industry as a subject for businessmen and trade unionists and with the support of notable industrialists he began the Economics Tripos in 1903.

Why should Cambridge have been so different from Oxford in its developments of science and a curriculum and research relevant to industry? We have seen that it was less reliant on Clarendon public schoolboy entrants and was more successful in transferring funds for science from the colleges to the university. To these may be added other factors. Cambridge had two Chancellors deeply committed to science – Prince Albert and the Duke of Devonshire. Also at Cambridge scholarships could be won after a years residence and students could change over to science at that point in spite of poor preparation at school. The basic culture of mathematics at Cambridge underpinned the sciences as classics at Oxford could not. The new sciences – the mathematical physics, engineering and even economics – were created by men who were expert Cambridge mathematicians before they developed their applied specialisms. Finally there was the luck of personalities. Oxford had the declining Odling and Clifton. Cambridge had Rayleigh, Thompson, Stuart, Ewing, Dewar and Stokes – five knights, a peer, two OMs, two Nobel prize winners and one Privy Councillor. This was an extraordinary cluster of talent in a university which numbered only 3,600 students by 1914. Rothblatt has pointed to a new sense of professionalism at Cambridge – a care about teaching, passion for research and scholarship, a concern to be useful and follow serious careers, eschewing donnish lazy self indulgence – a true 'revolution of the dons'

(Rothblatt, 1968). Accordingly the imbalance between Oxford and Cambridge in the provision of science and technology is reflected in their personnel in 1914. Oxford had 23 per cent of their faculty and 14 per cent of their students in science and technology; Cambridge had 37.3 and 35.4 per cent respectively (Roderick and Stephens, 1976).

The characters of Oxford and Cambridge were thus quite different, yet when we consider the social origins and future careers of Oxford and Cambridge men a further most important paradox emerges.

Male undergraduates coming from business backgrounds
as a percentage of all male students

Oxford			Cambridge			
(a)	1752–1886	0.1	(a)	1752–1886	9.4	
(c)	1900–13	28.8	(b)	1850–99	12	
			(e)	1900–14	19	(Sidney Sussex)

Male graduates going into business careers, as a percentage of all male students.

		per cent	
(a)	Oxford 1752–1886	0.6	
(d)	1870–1910	10–15	(Brasenose)
(d)	1883–1905	8	(Balliol)
(d)	1900s	9–14	(Appts Board)
(c)	1900–13	15.99	(Scientists)
(c)	1900–13	13.89	(Arts)
(a)	Cambridge 1752–1886	3.9	
(b)	1850–99	7	
(d)	1855–1900	15	(Jesus)
(d)	1885–1900	11.5	(Unspecified)

(a) Anderson and Schnaper (1952)
(b) Jenkins and Jones (1950)
(c) Harrison (1994)
(d) Sanderson (1972)
(e) Rothblatt (1968)

In the first three-quarters of the nineteenth century scarcely any businessmen's sons went to Oxford or Cambridge, though about 9 per cent of Cambridge students came from this background. Indeed Oxford and Cambridge had far fewer students coming from business backgrounds around 1880 (4 per cent) than major universities in Russia, Germany and the United States, but far more from nobility and gentry (33 per cent) and clergy (28 per cent) than any other (Anderson, 1959). Yet, whereas there was only a slight rise at Cambridge to the end of the century, there was a considerable change at Oxford, which totally overtook Cambridge as the fashionable university for businessmen whose sons made up over a quarter of undergraduates before 1914. Stone reciprocally notes that Oxford's reliance on gentry and clergy for its intake fell from 60 per cent in 1870 to 23 per cent by 1910 (Stone, 1974 p. 68). This increase in the number of businessmen's sons was in spite of the fact that there was very little that Oxford could offer the potential businessman. When we turn to the output from each university the paradox continues. As Oxford received few sons of businessmen before 1886 so it returned negligible proportions to such occupations. Oddly it produced more businessmen than it received, though the figures are so small that the point is of slight value. Cambridge even more oddly was sending half as many students to business than it received and must certainly have been diverting some to the Church and professions.

Yet by the end of the nineteenth century and the 1900s what is remarkable is that the outputs of Oxford and Cambridge are so similar in the 10–15 per cent range although both universities were so dissimilar in their suitability as educators of entrants to business and industry. It suggests that as fathers were looking for a social experience and status for their sons at Oxford, so business recruiters were seeking not so much relevant expertise as less definable social values. Indeed, that they accepted arts men as willingly as scientists from Oxford suggests this. They were probably looking for the kind of qualities in future managers that the Civil Service was selecting in its entrants. Lord Curzon, a leading Imperial proconsul and Chancellor of Oxford, welcomed Oxford graduates in Indian administration but considered that an Oxford degree ill equipped such men for business. He proposed a Diploma in Business at Oxford in 1914 but this was rejected (Symonds, 1986). The preference for Oxford among businessmen is seen in Rubinstein's analysis of the higher education of industrialists. He finds 6 per cent of leading industrialists in the

1900–19 period had been to Oxford but none to Cambridge (Rubinstein, 1986). For the rest of the century Cambridge became more important than Oxford as a supplier of leading industrialists but before 1914 it was not so. That British industry was neglecting or not attracting graduates from Cambridge and preferring that of Oxford – manifestly inferior in the quality and relevance of the education it provided – suggests a preference among industrial recruiters for social values at the expense of expertise and must be accounted a weakness in the formation of British industrial leadership.

5

Missed opportunities, 1914–1944

The period between the two World Wars was one in which nothing went seriously wrong as regards education and likewise the economic depression that generally pervaded these years can hardly be attributed to it. But nonetheless it was a period of wasted opportunities, when experiments failed or were abandoned, access to education remained painfully constricted and education ceased to be thought of as an important contributor to the economy. The Chief Inspector of Technical Education observed gloomily in 1933, that 'it is not generally believed that technical education can play a most important part in the struggle to increase the national well being; or if this belief is accepted, it does not generally lead to energetic action' (Abbott, 1933 p. 214). In this the period contrasts with the enthusiastic drive of the late Victorians and Edwardians, with their almost exaggerated belief in the importance of education, and also with the post World War II years which recovered something of the impetus but made more mistakes. The peacetime years of the twenties and thirties also contrast with the two World Wars which began and ended them when education received a powerful stimulus quite lacking in less urgent times.

The First World War years were good ones for education. In schooling there was a remarkable increase in the number of children going to grammar school from 187,000 in 1914 to 337,000 by 1920. There was ample employment, higher earnings and work for women and family budgets which experienced rising real wages for the first time since the 1890s. Working-class families could now afford to let children stay on into secondary education. The War itself brought home more urgently the importance of even basic literate and numerate skills. They were needed by truck drivers, map readers, gun layers and navigators at work. In leisure too the War stimulated the avid reading of newspapers. Soldiers at the front and loved ones at home maintained communication with more letter writing than they would have undertaken in peacetime while official forms and ration books required a reading comprehension and penmanship. A population which had achieved virtually total literacy by the 1900s found that the cruel circumstances of War confirmed the necessity of such skills and the new demands of wartime life must have forced many of the hesitantly near literate to new confidence and competency.

The War also raised expectations buoyed by the desire for more than an elementary education finishing at thirteen. In 1916 the 'Bradford Charter', drawn up by the Bradford Trades Council called for free and compulsory education up to sixteen, secondary education for all and continuation education for school leavers starting work. This became Labour Party policy in 1917 and much was adopted by the Liberals. Accordingly H. A. L. Fisher's Education Act of 1918 embodied many of these demands, raising the school leaving age to fourteen and providing for continuation schools influenced by the German Trade Continuation Schools of pre-War years. These developments would have boded well for an improved relationship of education and the economy had they not been overtaken by events.

The War also had a vitalising effect on the universities and their reputations. However indifferent many employers may have been to universities before the War the demands of War science gave new relevance to their work and a greater appreciation of their value. Universities were called upon to develop new war material. Explosives were tested on a regional basis at the universities of Manchester, Liverpool and Birmingham, who imposed rigorous standards of chemical consistency. Acetone for cordite and fabric dope for aircraft was developed by Chaim Weizmann at Manchester, tear gas at Imperial College and mustard gas by St Andrews, Manchester and Cambridge while defence against it with the gas mask owed much to work at Bristol and Birmingham. St Andrews was especially notable for the production of drugs, dulcitol for typhus, inulin for meningitis and novocaine anaesthetic. Some of the finest glass before 1914 had come from Germany, notably

Zeiss's optical glass for binoculars but Imperial College and Sheffield set to work to establish a scientific basis for our own glass industry. Dyes were another product for which we had been dependent on Germany and a leading part in replicating these was taken by Leeds and Manchester. In aeronautics Imperial College and Bristol were prominent while wireless was developed at University College London and Royal Holloway College, wireless signalling to submarines at Birmingham and submarine detection at Queen Mary College.

These activities were significant in various ways. Firstly the War forced British industry to produce products formerly imported from Germany – the dyes, drugs, magnetos and even washing powder. Secondly this was usually achieved by the co-operation of universities and industrial firms like British Dyes, Metropolitan Vickers and Nobels bringing a greater appreciation of practical manufacture to universities and making firms more aware of the importance of science, research and university graduates. In turn it transformed certain universities. The major civics in industrial cities had always been closely linked with industry but now formerly rather disengaged institutions like St Andrews (through its drugs) and Bangor (through its work on magnetos and aviation) found new relevance in their work. Thirdly this concern with war industry and science brought a closer relation of the universities and government through the Department of Scientific and Industrial Research, the Ministry of Munitions, the Board of Trade and the research associations of various industries. It gave the universities more credibility in government circles and at the end of the War the Advisory Committee on University Grants became the University Grants Committee channelling increased government money to universities. Fourthly the War proved that when necessary British industry, and the education behind it, could very rapidly match and even surpass the German products on which we had been so dependent. Within a year and a half or so we were making our own magnetos, pharmaceuticals, dyes and glass. Our steel helmets had more bullet resistance than the Germans, our uniforms were tougher, our aeroplanes more stable, our novocaine anaesthetic more pain deadening and our mustard gas cheaper. The rapid catching up with the Germans and the close alignment of education in support of wartime industry is a strong circumstantial argument in the optimist case that before 1914 it was an exaggeration to attribute relative retardation to defects in education.

With the start of the interwar years a number of things began to go wrong or hoped-for developments which might have helped industry did not materialise. The Fisher Act of 1918 raised the school leaving age to fourteen but also required Local Education Authorities to provide Continuation Schools. These were to give part-time education for 320 hours a year for adolescents up to the age of sixteen (and ultimately to eighteen it was hoped) who had already started work. It would widen their education and enhance their skills. The Continuation Schools, in conjunction with the Junior Technical Schools would have replicated the features of the German Trade Continuation Schools (*Fortbildungschulen*) so admired before the War. This would have been a valuable link between industry and schooling (Dean, 1970; Sherington, 1981). But it was not to be. A few schools were created, notably in West Ham and Rugby, but financial cuts in 1921 and 1922 put paid to their general expansion. Only Rugby fulfilled the requirements of the Act since the schools were especially appropriate for the apprentices of British Thomson Houston and the railway workshops which were prominent industries of the town. The future of the Day Continuation Schools lay with some private firms rather than the LEA. Some firms like Metropolitan Vickers, Cadburys and Boots ran their own. It was thought that about 100 employers had adopted such schemes but these were usually for general education rather than technical training to enhance skill.

Things fared scarcely better with the Junior Technical Schools started with such hopes before the War. Their expansion was only modest from 37 in 1914 to 248 by 1938 (Bailey, 1990). But even by the 1930s they took only 2.6 per cent of boys and 1.4 per cent of girls of JTS schooling age. Various factors lay behind the failure of the JTS to develop. Firstly they were expensive to build and equip. They required workshops with expensive machinery and reinforced structures capable of receiving bulk and weight. Even commercially oriented JTSs needed large rooms full of typewriters and business equipment. Accordingly such schools were consistently more costly than grammar schools to build and to run. It was a curious paradox that schools designed for the working classes who had failed the 11-plus examination should prove more expensive for the ratepayers than the grammar schools for those who had passed. It was not surprising that most LEAs preferred not to have JTSs or to provide them only as subsections of Technical Colleges. Second the JTS fitted awkwardly into the existing structures of selection and allocation to post-elementary education. After the 11-plus academic children were allocated to grammar schools and the less good to central or senior schools and failures back to all-age primary schools whence they had come. However the age of entry to the JTS was thirteen and not eleven. The reasons for this were twofold. It was not thought desirable that pre-adolescents should be pre-empted into specific trades such as engineering and construction as early as eleven to the detriment of their general education. Also whereas psychologists believed that it was possible to test and discern intelligence at the age of eleven they did not believe that technical aptitudes became manifest until the age of thirteen. Accordingly children not academically good enough for grammar schools had to be decanted into other post-eleven schools before being re-decanted into the JTSs, where available, two years later. This was administratively messy and most Chief Education Officers preferred not to trouble with it.

Thirdly, the JTSs received no strong support from employers. Some industries had no use for them – textiles, chemicals, coal mining. They were valued by engineers especially in Lancashire and Yorkshire and by certain specialised trades notably in London – photography and silversmithing for example. But the general depression of the inter-war years and the high levels of unemployment even in areas of industry for which JTSs trained labour removed much urgency to produce even more. Similarly, contempt for a recently defeated Germany replaced that admiration with which it had been regarded and which had motivated much British industrial concern for technical education before 1914. The Left disliked JTSs. Ideologists like R. H. Tawney and Albert Mansbridge suspected them as directing working-class children too early into manual though skilled working-class jobs. This denied them the more general education which was their due. Such views were significant since both Tawney and Mansbridge were members of the Hadow Committee whose report in 1926 was the basis of the restructuring of education into primary and various types of secondary school and which took a very negative view of the JTSs. Also the trade unions did not like JTSs either. For them they threatened to over-produce engineers and builders which would drive down the wages of such skilled men yet further in time of depression. The Conservative middle class conversely were quite indifferent to JTSs. For them technical education was inferior to the arts and sciences taught at the public and grammar schools attended by their children. They wanted their rates to be spent on the grammar school expansion of the 1930s not on more expensive schools for social inferiors. Thus a mixture of financial prudence, administrative difficulties, industrial apathy, class suspicions and the overriding prestige of liberal education stifled forms of schooling where education and industry could have drawn closer to the benefit of the latter (Sanderson, 1994).

The generally depressed state of the economy in the interwar years also had stultifying effects on education which in turn limited its potential contribution back to the economy itself. Successive economic crises held back any onward momentum in developing the system. Scarcely had the Fisher Act begun to be implemented than post-war recession led to cuts in education in January and August 1921 and then with Sir Eric Geddes 'axe' on public expenditure which cut £18 million from education in 1922–3. This swept away any hopes of raising the school-leaving age to fifteen, reduced teachers' salaries, increased class sizes and cut state scholarships to universities (Simon, 1974). It was at this time that education acts were no longer regarded as legislation which governments were bound to honour since the retreat from statute law could be effected by departmental orders. More was to come. As the Conservatives returned in 1924 with Churchill concerned to depress the price level as part of his policy of returning to the gold standard, so further cuts followed in November 1925. The world slump inevitably prompted further setbacks. The May Committee 1931 called for more public spending cuts and education bore the brunt. Again plans to raise the school-leaving age were abandoned, teachers' salaries were cut, 'free place' scholarships to grammar schools were replaced by means tested 'special' places. Although salary cuts were restored in 1935 attempts to raise the school-leaving age by the

Oliver Stanley Act in 1936 were overtaken by the outbreak of War.

The depression also warped the relationship of local authorities and families to education. Over the interwar years the LEAs overtook central government as the dominant partner in the finance of education. Yet in depressed years and depressed areas since LEAs had to rely on their own resources so a vicious circle was set up. In depressed areas with poor housing, low rateable values and unemployed populations the take up of rate money was inevitably limited. But in such places the greatest call on that money was unemployment benefit. Since unemployment benefit and education were the two largest outlays of local government spending then that on education was consequently curtailed. This meant that fewer grammar schools, JTSs and technical colleges could be built, precisely those educational institutions which would channel the ablest working-class youth from unemployment to productive work – from being drains on public expenditure to being contributors to it.

Also depression distorted the decisions of poor working-class families about education. A grammar school scholarship would be the passport to the School Certificate, university or safe respectable white-collar jobs in banks, building societies and the offices of solicitors and accountants. Yet many poor families would see the grammar school as a threat to their financial stability rather than a long-term opportunity. There were the hidden costs of uniforms, books and stationery. Even more important there was the foregone income of grammar school pupils. Since such pupils were expected to stay until sixteen they lost the job opportunities of fourteen to sixteen-year-olds, who were attractive to employers since they did not entail national insurance costs. The rejection of grammar school places even by families whose children had won scholarships – 60 per cent in Bradford – represented a waste of ability.

The depression deflated many of the pressures that would have expanded or improved the system. Few politicians especially of the first rank espoused the cause of education. Labour understandably saw problems of the economy, poverty and unemployment as taking precedence. Whereas education had been seen by politicians before 1914 as a panacea for almost all problems, by the interwar years it had almost ceased to matter. The high levels of unemployment even of skilled men and their ready and cheap availability removed much urgency to train even more of them. The lack of urgency about skill creation is reflected in the rate of growth of quality shift in the labour force, that is the movement of workers from low-paid to high-paid jobs. This fell to only 0.05 per cent per annum in the period 1924–37 compared with 0.1 per cent in the period 1871–1911 and a much higher 0.17 per cent between 1951 and 1973 (Burgess, 1994 citing N. F. R. Crafts). The depression also lowered the birthrate as families sought to defend their standard of living, or prevent a headlong fall into poverty by restricting the size of their families. For the first time since the early eighteenth century the education system was no longer driven by the need to cater for rising numbers of children, as it had most notably been in Victorian times. Also as the admiration of Germany had been removed as a positive factor in educational development so foreign policy and defence fears came to work against education. Defence expenditure was regularly about twice that on education from 1921–1935 and then about three times as great for the rest of the 1930s.

The result of these depressive factors was a very constrained flow of talent through the education system. One of the achievements of the 1930s was the reorganisation of secondary education on the lines proposed by the Hadow Report in 1926. This was that 'secondary education for all' should replace the situation in which most children received only elementary education. Hadow's intention was that after the age of eleven children should receive a secondary education in a secondary 'grammar' school or in some more specialised technical school. LEAs were encouraged to build secondary schools to receive these post-11 pupils and to raise the proportion of grammar school places reserved for ex-elementary children from 25 per cent, as it had been from the 1900s to 40 per cent, as had been recommended by the Labour government in 1924. There was a modest increase in secondary schools from 1,301 in 1926 to 1,398 by 1939 and a greater one in pupils from 360,503 in 1926 to 470,003 by 1939. The result too was modest with ex-elementary school children admitted to secondary schools rising, within low levels, from 10 per cent in 1931 to 14 per cent by 1938 (Simon, 1974, p. 366). Put another way – in 1922 only 7.2 per cent of children aged eleven to sixteen were in secondary schools and this had risen to only 9.9 per cent by 1937 (San-derson, 1987 p. 29).

What also concerned contemporaries was the low level of access of working-class children to grammar schools. The percentage of children of semi- and unskilled fathers achieving grammar school places rose from 1 per cent for those born before 1910 to 4 per cent for those born between 1910 and 1919 and to 7 per cent for those born in the period from 1920 to 1929 (Little and Wester-gaard, 1964). It was a decent rise but from the miniscule to the very small. Most damning was the finding that 73 per cent of children of high intelligence over the age of eleven were still in elementary schools or in central schools in 1935 and destined to leave at fourteen or fifteen in 1935 (Gray and Moshinsky, 1935). Conversely 49 per cent of fee-paying children in grammar schools were not of the intelligence to benefit from such education. Thus even in the 1930s the unintelligent well-to-do were cluttering up grammar schools supposedly for the academically highly intelli-gent, while three-quarters of the stock of the nation's high intelligence were in schools where they would leave early, not become graduates and serve industry at the level appropriate to their abilities. There was also another mis-conjunction in that boys coming from industrial and manual working backgrounds who got to grammar schools tended not to go into industrial careers but become schoolteachers. They will have seen this as an advance in life and derived career satisfaction from it but it might have been to industry's advantage if lads from such a background had returned to it but at a much higher level.

The lack of much flow from elementary schools to grammar schools was mirrored in that to higher education. The university population rose from around 40,000 to 50,000 in the interwar years, most of the increase coming over the turn of the decades, probably as a result of students seeking universities as a refuge from unemployment. Only 1.5 per cent of eighteen-year-olds went to university in 1924/5 and 1.7 per cent by 1938/9 (Robbins, 1963 p. 16). Within these tiny figures only 1.5 per cent of boys of manual skilled, semi- and unskilled workers born pre-1910 and only 2.5 per cent of those born in the 1920s went to university. No girls of the same classes achieved this in either period (Little and Westergaard, 1964 p. 310).

This was on the low side by European comparisons. In 1930 the United Kingdom secondary school pupil ratio was 1.26 per cent of the population compared with 1.54 in Germany and 1.34 in the Netherlands. We were better than France, which did not raise its school leaving age to fourteen until Leon Blum's administration in 1936. The 1.5 and 1.7 percentages for the proportion of British eighteen-year-olds entering universities cited above compare with a German 2.7 per cent for 1921 and 1931, a French 2.0 and 2.9 for 1921 and 1931. Although Britain remained the richest country in Europe yet its educational levels were not at the forefront. It was as if there was little belief that economic advantage could be used to sustain an educational one for the future. The real danger of this, as Lars Sandberg as shown (Sandberg, 1982) is that educational rankings rarely match economic rankings at the same point in time but that educational rankings uncannily foreshadow (determine?) economic rankings of the future.

It is of course harsh to judge even the recent past by the standards of the present when everyone receives a secondary education and – post Dearing – it is assumed that half the population should soon be attending university. But the very low proportions of the population for whom secondary and higher education were available in the interwar years, the slight changes within tiny percentages, the difficulties of even very able working-class children in moving through the system, the cavalier misallocation of high ability made possible by allowing fee payers to buy places in grammar schools which they were inappropriate to hold, the modest performance in relation to other leading European countries – all suggest a wastefulness in the formation of human capital in Britain at the heart of the twentieth century which was to do the economy no good.

If we focus on industrial training specifically there were a number of questionable defects highlighted by observers at the time. It was evident that there was a change in skill levels in engineering. C. G. Renold noted that in his firm there had been a marked reduction in the need for semi-skilled machine operators, unskilled labourers and even managers, but a sharp increase in the need for skilled craftsmen who at 15.9 per cent of his labour force were a larger proportion than any other category except women clerks (Renold, 1928).

Yet where was such skill to be trained? There were good arguments why training within the firm was becoming less appropriate. With mass production, works were less able to train workers as the division of labour became more fragmented in contrast with the old craft system. It would also throw the product line out of time to take a youth between processes and machines. Moreover as workmen were generally paid piece work, time given to training a lad would diminish an adult worker's earnings. The head of a leading technical college, who made the foregoing observations, noted that 'training and production will separate more and more' (Richardson, 1939).

This placed more onus on the technical college and these institutions had several characteristics both remarkable and questionable. It was estimated that one in fifteen workers in the late 1930s were engaged in some form of part-time education – 'this is astonishing' (Richardson, 1939 p. 23). Yet the bulk of such education was in evening classes either at the technical college or in evening institutes. Day students at technical colleges were only 22,000 in 1921 and although these had doubled by 1938 they were still dwarfed by the 1,280,000 part timers. Critics thought that it was inefficient to expect tired young workers to learn effectively at night after work and that without compulsory day release 'the technical college will continue to be a night school'. Indeed the witticism was that the 'T' (Technical) branch of the Board of Education 'stood for everything after tea' (McCormick, 1986). The difficulties of studying might also be suggested by the reception of the Ordinary and Higher National Diplomas. These had been introduced in 1920 as new technical qualifications to raise standards, yet by 1938 there had been only 3317 successes at ONC and 1668 at HNC (Albu, 1980) small figures compared even with those of day students at technical colleges.

The day release of workers to study at the 'tech' during the working day was very variable differing from 60 per 1,000 in printing and 58 in chemicals, 43 in engineering down through a mean of 23 to the lower reaches with mining with 6 and textiles with 4. On the whole it was modern 'new' industries and those dependent on science and research, 'that are most anxious to educate their people and place some value on education' (Richardson, 1939 p. 368). On the other hand it was the older industries complaining of difficult times which 'are suffering from the lack of educated personnel' (Richardson, 1939 p. 368). There was a similar variability in industries taking apprentices, as shown by the monumental Inquiry into Apprenticeship and Training in the mid-1920s. Here the percentage of firms recruiting apprentices spanned from 20 per cent in electrical supply and gas engineering through 11 per cent in shipbuilding and foundry work through to very few in glass, furniture and hosiery. The other 80 per cent of firms and more presumably poached their labour from the minority of trainers (Sanderson, 1994 p. 80).

The Balfour Committee of 1925–6, reporting at about the same time, also took a cool view of industrial training. They found that the depressed state of the economy had led to low levels of apprenticeship. Although there were some more flexible five-year learnerships the rigid seven-year apprenticeship largely remained. Mechanisation and the division of labour was reducing the need for such trained men and larger firms were not training but pirating skilled labour while day release was granted by very few. Balfour concluded that 'so far as manual workers were concerned, training was in decline' (Evans and Wiseman, 1984). Roderick and Stephens also take a bleak view of this period, 'firms were not interested in the education of their employees and the few firms involved were only interested in part-time evening instruction and not in the new day-release schemes. There was little contact between schools and industry as teaching was thought by industrialists to be too academic and theoretical' (Roderick and Stephens, 1982 p. 25).

Another defect in these arrangements was the curious gap between the school leaving age of fourteen and the eligibility for unemployment insurance at sixteen. In this interim a youth need not be at school, but neither need he visit a Labour Exchange, it was not necessary to know or record whether he was unemployed. The danger of this was the drifting into dead-end jobs since industries were unable to absorb as adults all those it required as juveniles. The gap also enticed children to leave school early since employers were happy to employ juveniles on low wages and with no insurance stamp. The perils of the gap were also compounded by the tendency for skilled trades to raise their age of entry for apprenticeship to sixteen. They might prefer the intelligent disciplined youth straight from school, and with more mathematics, than one who had left elementary school at fourteen and languished in the dead-end gap for two years. It was remarkable that nothing was done about it possibly because of the constant and frustrated expectations that the school-leaving age would shortly be raised. But it was yet another area of waste in the formation of skill in these years.

Yet it has been argued that criticising the provision of technical education in this period is beside the point since employers did not require it (Burgess, 1994). For example an Engineering Training Organisation was formed in 1917 but collapsed in 1920, only 30 of the 226 firms invited to do so having become members. Also only 8.3 per cent of employers in a British Association for Commercial and Industrial Education survey in 1936 favoured vocational education before the age of sixteen. Employers were more concerned that schools provide personal qualities of initiative and character, commitment to the institution and interpersonal sociability. Also they preferred to select employees on non credentialist criteria and train them themselves. There is a subtle laying off of blame here as Burgess perceptively points out. The Board of Education can hardly be criticised for not providing a technical education for schoolchildren which employers did not really want. But they may have failed to recognise the employers' needs for personal rather than technical capabilities. On the other hand again were the employers right to take this 'soft' attitude to technical training? Burgess concludes that they had only themselves to blame – 'it was the experience of British employers themselves that made them neglectful of skill formation relevant to the productive economy' and these attitudes carried over into the post-war years.

Keeble too places much of the blame on employers for defects in the education–industry link on the latter in these years. Employers opposed continuation education in the Fisher Act and did not do enough to sustain the form themselves when it became evident that government both central and local, could not do so. They backed the cheap form of all-age elementary schools taking pupils until the age of fourteen rather than proper secondary education. Secondary education provided education of a 'wider scope and more advanced degree than that given in elementary schools' as the 1904 Regulations for Secondary Schools put it. The all-age elementary schools were accordingly denied that widening curriculum of the interwar secondary schools – modern languages, economics, biology let alone more advanced science. Above all the secondary school led to the School Certificate (from 1917) and the university matriculation examinations as the elementary schools could not. Employers were less concerned about this than the cheaper costs of elementary schools and the strong likelihood that their local elementary school would receive a higher proportion of its income from the central exchequer than the corresponding secondary school (Simon, 1974 pp. 360–1). Employers also failed to support the junior technical schools which might have been in their interests and they tended to regard education as part of 'welfare', only something to be afforded when times were prosperous but not an investment to draw the economy out of depression. At one with this attitude they preferred employees to take vocational examinations in their own time and at their own expense. They believed that such education benefited individuals but 'it does not enter their minds that such schools might aid their industries' (Keeble, 1992, chapter 4 'The British Rejection of Formal Education'). Such attitudes and deficiencies were part of the weaknesses in technical and vocational training which may have been an element in the productivity gap between Britain and the United States in the 1930s. United States productivity was twice that of Britain and this gap 'was the result of lower British human capital' (Broadberry and Crafts, 1992 p. 553).

The contribution of the universities to industry was creditable as various factors pushed the two together. The rise of research laboratories within the firm and the DSIR research laboratories created a demand for more science graduates. Universities had started PhD work during the War since it was no longer possible for British graduates to visit Germany for such studies as had been customary before 1914. Also the increasing concentration, rationalisation and mergers in industry demanded a higher level of ability from future senior managers. The pause in recruitment during the War had left an age imbalance of older managers and youthful newcomers in the 1920s. As the ageing senior figures came to retire they looked to able mature graduates who could rise swiftly to replace them rather than to ex-elementary or even secondary school boys.

Many universities played their part in helping to develop the 'new' industries which modernised Britain's industrial structure. Manchester, in conjunction with the British Dyestuffs Corporation laboratories at Blackley, helped to revive the dyestuffs industry and the new ICI formed from the alkali firms of the Mersey basin called on both Manchester and Liverpool for graduates and science. Liverpool also developed special fortes in fat chemistry and refrigeration necessary for the port and local firms such as Lever Bros. Aviation found support from Imperial College as Churchill had wished while Birmingham made itself a centre for oil geology. Bristol cornered the market in work on certain food products, jam canning, cider, perry and cheese. And there were many more (Sanderson, 1972).

In university engineering education Divall finds a good match between what was provided and what employers required (Divall, 1990). Various reasons lay behind this. By the late 1920s an undergraduate education had largely replaced pupillage in the offices of a leading engineer as the training route taken by the higher social classes into engineering. Moreover the professional associations of engineers such as the Institution of Civil Engineers and newcomers like the Municipal Engineers sought to increase their membership by taking graduates in engineering, all by 1914. They accordingly accepted university degrees as exemptions from their own examinations which were designed originally for non-graduate pupils. But as they accepted degrees, so they influenced their content as a condition of that acceptance, and in this way employers 'enjoyed a considerable if largely benign influence on the curriculum acting principally through the professional institutions'. This was especially valuable since professors of engineering rarely had much industrial experience and had little influence on the councils of the institutions. So in this way the disciplines of the industrial employer were imposed on the academics through the institutions and reflected in the degree curricula. Also the universities provided a range of approaches from the 'high academic' mathematical and theoretical of Cambridge to the practicalities of the Manchester College of Technology. The 'high academic' was favoured by the electrical, aircraft and electrical engineering firms for whom research was important; the more practical by the municipal and sanitary engineers. So 'a basic understanding had been reached between the universities and the institutions over the curriculum' (Divall, 1990 p. 90).

Expressed in these terms the picture appears an optimistic one but there were a number of grounds for unease. Firstly there was a sharp decline in the proportion of technology students and a commensurate rise in arts graduates.

	Arts	Pure science	Technology
1920/1–1924/5	39.8	17.0	13.5
1935/6–1938/9	46.5	16.3	9.7

Reflecting this, of the seventy-one new chairs created between 1925 and 1930 only four were in technology compared with fifteen in mathematics and science and thirty-nine in arts (Roderick and Stephens, 1982 p. 24). Secondly there were some significant mismatches in the universities' supply of what industry needed. In some areas the universities did not produce sufficient types of industrial skill. For example 4,167 chemists were produced between 1926 and 1939 but only 300 chemical engineers whose persistent undersupply was complained of. A general degree in chemistry was preferred as leading to a schoolteaching career in those insecure times and universities were probably wary of the high expense of running a chemical engineering department especially since there was little student demand for it. Metallurgists too were remarkably undersupplied, about fifteen a year in the late 1920s and mid-1930s. A third surprising neglect was that of graduates suitable for geology in the oil industry. There were ten coal-mining departments – excessive to some expert observers and twice as many as those in Germany. Yet only Birmingham seriously diversified into metal ore mining and oil geology and too few school-leavers took up these studies.

There was also a disengagement in electrical engineering. Universities continued to produce routine electrical engineers satisfactorily. There was even a shift from mechanical engineering, seen as associated with traditional old industries, to electrical engineering as one of the fastest growing new ones. Yet as regards research, universities became much less important than they had been in the 1890s and 1900s. There were two main reasons for this. First the electrical firms now tended to do their own research in the great laboratories, GEC at Wembley and Metro-Vickers at Trafford Park, rather than rely on university departments. Secondly, the nuclear physics of the Cavendish Laboratory in Cambridge came to dominate fashion in the other universities as Cavendish fellows took chairs in the provinces. Valuable as this later was in providing a team to work on the atomic bomb it disengaged much university physics from the practical engineering problems of manufacturing industry until the nuclear reactors of the 1950s.

Finally there was a decline in the relation of the Scottish universities to industry. Their technology students fell from 17.9 per cent in 1920/1 to 8.9 per cent by 1938/9. The special prestige of the big Scottish technical colleges – the Royal Technical College in Glasgow (later University of Strathclyde) and Heriot Watt College (later University) in Edinburgh – removed some urgency from universities proper to cater for technologies closely related to industry. Also Scottish university technology departments were related to old industries of mining, marine engineering and shipbuilding where the slump in students reflected that of employment prospects. Scotland did not develop new industries such as aircraft, motor cars or even electrical engineering to the extent of England.

The impact of the interwar years depression on the public schools was a mixed one as regards their relevance to the economy. The decline of the birth rate, especially among the middle classes, as well as the dangers of unemployment posed a serious threat to the public schools who feared and experienced a loss of clientele. 263 preparatory schools went out of business though no Headmasters' Conference School failed to survive. But the implications for their role in serving the economy were two-fold. Firstly many schools survived by raising their fees and extending their curricula notably into modern languages and improving their science facilities with considerable building expansion. The HMC contacted 153 member schools and practically all reported that they had engaged in large-scale building in the 1930s. But the recession had a short-term effect in diverting boys' choice of careers away from industry and commerce and towards the 'safe' professions. For example at Winchester (Bishop and Wilkinson, 1967) and similar trends are evident at Bradfield, Epsom, Durham, Gresham's Holt and Aldenham (Sanderson, 1997). This may have temporarily deprived the economy of a cohort of ability after a long period in which public school boys showed a greater inclination to take up such productive careers.

Occupations of boys leaving Winchester *c.*1918–40

born leaving school	1900–9 1918–27	1910–19 1928–37	1920–2 1938–40
careers in business industry engineering	32.2	22.3	7.2
'safe' professions (clergy, medical, teaching, civil service, armed forces)	38.1	57.1	84.3

As the First World War had vitalised education and its contribution to the economy so too did the Second. University scientists played a vital part in the creation of military technologies that were to develop into industries after the War. The atomic bomb derived ultimately from the nuclear physics developed at the Cavendish Laboratory from the 1890s. This expertise, built up in the inter-war years, spread through other universities forming a body of professors who could be assembled by Sir John Cockcroft to work on the bomb. Civil industrial atomic energy subsequently arose from the work of British scientists at Chalk River in Canada and it was from discussions there that Harwell was established under Cockcroft. Accordingly academic science of the pre-war years had led to practical military engineering and in turn to a major new peacetime industry and source of energy.

A second major area where universities created a new industry was radar. Here again Cockcroft gathered physicists who could work on radar which was being developed by Robert Watson Watt. Oxford was important here and also Birmingham where Sir Marcus Oliphant's team created the cavity magnetron while the klystron valve came from Bristol University. This activity brought a closer liaison between universities and the electrical industry than had existed before the War. In a whole range of other areas, radio, operational research, methane fuel, synthetic rubber, penicillin and scores of others university scientists were helping to create and develop products and industries, as they had in the First World War.

In turn the greater appreciation of the role of the universities and scientists and industry led to calls for a substantial increase in university students in the post-war years. The Percy Committee in 1945 noted the rise in output of engineers from an annual 700 pre-war to 3,000 a year post-1943 and called for the sustaining of the wartime figure into peacetime. The Barlow Committee also of 1945 estimated that there were 60,000 qualified scientists in Britain in 1945 and that this would rise to 90,000 by 1955. A doubling of the output of scientists from the universities from 2,500 to 5,000 would be necessary to effect this. This in turn questioned the 2 per cent of population going to university as being too low especially since 5 per cent of the population possessed intelligence as high as the upper half of university students. The urgency of the War had created new expectations of the relevance of education to the economy and broken some of the complacent and restrictive attitudes of the inter-war years.

Some of this new wartime spirit was caught in R. A. Butler's Education Act of 1944. This raised the school-leaving age to fifteen – an expectation of H. A. L. Fisher which had been constantly frustrated in the inter-war years. Most important, it abolished fee paying and stationery costs in grammar schools. This was intended to remove the anomalies of the inter-war years whereby able poor children declined places which were then filled by children of wealthier backgrounds who could pay fees but who were not of the intelligence to benefit from an academic education. The Butler Act required LEAs to provide an education appropriate to a child's 'age, ability and aptitude' but did not specify that this had to be in the familiar tripartite form of grammar school, technical school and secondary modern. This left flexibility for the introduction of multilateral or comprehensive schools. But since the building stock that most LEAs already owned embodied a tripartite division inherited from Morant's day, this shaped the manner in which the Act would generally be implemented. The post-war years accordingly began in an atmosphere of idealistic optimism that could not long be sustained or justified.

6

Post-war decline – the betrayed teenager?

The post-war years saw a revival of preoccupation with decline, so important in the rhetoric of the late Victorians and Edwardians but less so in the inter-war years. Tomlinson sees this revival of concern as dating from the late 1950s and early 1960s (Tomlinson, 1996). The need to modernise became an issue in successive general elections as the party out of office could gain political advantage by accusing the incumbent government for failing to 'catch up' on some 'falling behind'. Statisticians began to compile systematic data on national income and national product from the 1950s making comparisons possible between Britain and competitor countries. Also 'productivity' to which much attention had been paid in wartime came to be regarded as yet another criterion of performance in the 1950s. Behind that was the belief that quality of manpower, or 'human capital' as it was called in the early 1960s was an element in productivity and hence in growth performance. The growing interest in the economics of under-developed countries in the 1950s also focused attention on education as an element in growth. Accordingly from the 1950s and 1960s revived attention was paid to education in the belief that its defects contributed to decline or that its reform could allay it.

In the post-war years Britain's poor economic performance became more marked. The United Kingdom's regular 2.5–3 per cent growth compared modestly with France's 4–6 per cent, Germany's 4–9 per cent, the United States' normal 4 per cent, let alone Japan's 7–11 per cent. It could have been argued in the immediate post-war years that war-damaged countries were bound to show higher growth rates than Britain as the former recovered from artificially low levels (see table 6.1). But from the early 1960s

Table 6.1 Post-war average annual growth of GDP in selected trading nations

| | Average annual percentage growth of GDP | | | | |
	1950–5	1955–60	1960–4	1965–69	1969–73
UK	2.9	2.5	3.1	2.5	3.0
France	4.4	4.8	6.0	5.9	6.1
Germany	9.1	6.4	5.1	4.6	4.5
Japan	7.1	9.0	11.7	10.9	9.3
USA	4.2	2.4	4.4	4.3	4.4

Source: Alford, (1988) p. 14 citing Sir Alec Cairncross and D. T. Jones.

this excuse became less credible. Although the competitor nations all experienced a slackening of growth rates after the early sixties so did the United Kingdom and at a markedly lower level.

Of course it would be nonsense to attribute all this slow growth to defects of education. There were many causes of it – the low rate of investment, the oil-price rises, the demand management policies leading to booms and slumps with attendant restrictions, high levels of public expenditure especially in defence as we sought to maintain a defence capability beyond our means, an over-large public sector, excessive taxation, too many 'sleeper' managers and entrepreneurs and too few 'thrusters' (Aldcroft, 1982). Yet near the heart of the low growth was Britain's low productivity which suggested defects in the levels of skill and hence in levels of education and training. However, Derek Aldcroft points out that United Kingdom expenditure has not been out of line with other countries as its growth and productivity levels have been (Aldcroft, 1992).

Table 6.2 Growth in labour productivity GDP per hour worked, average annual compound growth rate

	1950–73	1973–83
UK	3.2	2.4
France	5.1	3.4
West Germany	6.0	3.0
Japan	7.7	3.2
Five country average	5.3	2.8
USA	2.5	1.0

Expenditure on education has been 5 or 6 per cent of GNP in the 1960s–80s which is consistent with that of most advanced countries whose spending is in the 4–7 per cent range. Indeed United Kingdom proportions have been slightly ahead of France, Germany and Japan. So if there was nothing peculiarly poor about our expenditure then have defects in educational policy been to blame?

The post-war years began with the optimism of hopes invested in the Butler Act. This raised the school-leaving age from fourteen to fifteen from 1 April 1947. Its immediate effect was adverse for the economy since it held back in school 350,000 juveniles who might have joined the labour market. It left the cotton industry 11,000 short and hosiery 9,000 and in a context in which there was very little juvenile unemployment it pushed up juvenile earnings by 10 per cent between June 1947 and October 1948 (O'Keefe, 1975). Very few economists, except Sir Hubert Henderson, had foreseen this or were concerned about it. It did cause a temporary setback but could hardly be seen as a long-term drag on the economy. Most agreed that it would be quickly offset by an improvement in the quality of better (or at least longer) schooled juvenile workers. In any case there was a revulsion against employing youth in early adolescence as there had been against child labour in Victorian times. Criticisms of the Butler Act were to lie elsewhere.

Doubts arose about the implementation of the 1944 Act on two grounds; it led to too much wastage of ability and it under-estimated the importance of technical education. Both deficiencies were to prove drawbacks in the formation of a labour force appropriate for industry. It soon became evident that the operation of the 11-plus examination allocating children to grammar schools, secondary modern schools and a few secondary technical schools had not led to much more 'capacity catching' than before, in spite of the abolition of fees in grammar schools. In a classic study in the 1950s Jean Floud, A. H. Halsey and Frank Martin studied Middlesbrough and South West Hertfordshire to examine whether access to grammar schools had improved for the working classes since the inter-war years. Their conclusion was modest: 'the likelihood that a working class boy will reach a grammar school is not notably greater today, despite all the changes than it was before 1945. Rather less than ten per cent of working-class boys reaching the age of eleven in the years 1931–41 entered selective secondary schools. In 1953 in South West Hertfordshire the proportion was 15.5 per cent and in Middlesbrough 12 per cent.' (Floud, Halsey, Martin, 1956 p. 33). The lack of change since the inter-war years was confirmed in a later study by A. H. Halsey who interviewed 8,529 men in 1972 and found that, whereas 20.2 per cent of working-class men entered selective secondary schools in the period 1924–33, this had scarcely changed to 21.6 per cent by 1954–93 (Halsey, Heath and Ridge, 1980). In the 1950s Floud and Halsey had placed an optimistic interpretation on their findings. Far from regarding it as evidence of injustice they pointed out that judged by the proportion of any social class likely to have an IQ of 114.2 (that supposedly required for grammar school entry) then 'the distribution of opportunity stands in closer relationship to that of ability than ever before'.

Greater unease arose in the 1960s as it became evident that all kinds of environmental and psychological factors were throwing doubt on the efficiency of the selection system (Douglas, 1964). First, regional variations in the supply of grammar schools proved to be almost the most important factor determining the pass rate of the 11-plus. The chances of getting a grammar school place in 1959 ranged from the highest 35 per cent in South West England to the lowest 18.9 per cent a few miles to the east in the centre South of England. Industrial areas like the North East and the Midlands provided rather low chances of 22.4 per cent and 24 per cent respectively. Second J. W. B. Douglas drew attention to the role of the home and especially the influence of the mother in a child's chances of reaching the grammar school. 73.3 per cent of upper-middle-class mothers wanted a grammar school place for their child compared with 48.8 per cent of lower-working-class mothers. And there were even wider disparities between social classes in showing a high interest in school progress or wanting the child to stay on into the sixth form. The implications of this were that maternal attitudes could influence a child for good or ill between the ages of 8 and 11 as they approached the 11-plus examination. Accordingly what was being selected was as much the social-class attitudes of the mother as the intelligence of the child.

Thirdly there was unease about the nature of the test itself. The arithmetic and intelligence parts of the test were regarded as fair but the English component was thought to favour children from middle-class backgrounds who had aquired a range of vocabulary and fluency in grammar less from school than from their home backgrounds. This was a bias even against intelligent working-class children. Moreover the 11-plus was regarded as good at finding future clerks, civil servants and schoolteachers but less so at detecting future engineers and businessmen especially since there was no aptitude element in the test. Worst of all there was ambivalence about the role of the 11-plus. Was it an absolute standard finding children of an IQ of 114.2 who would be fit to go to grammar school or was it merely creaming off as many children as there were available grammar school places in any LEA irrespective of their IQ? It was obviously the latter. Otherwise one had to marvel that in every town in every year there were always just enough desks and chairs in each grammar school throughout the land to receive those with an IQ of 114.2 and that this never varied even with year to year fluctuations in the numbers of eleven year olds. One would also have to believe that children in Devon were consistently twice as intelligent as those in Hampshire. There were also other concerns – the low intelligence of late-born children in large families, the pre-emptive streaming from the age of seven which created self fulfilling prophesies of who would pass at eleven, the fairly wide range of those taking the test (from 10 years 6 months to 11 years 5 months). The outcome of all this, as the Crowther Report found was that 22 per cent of army and 20 per cent of RAF recruits had been allocated to schools lower than their ability warranted (Crowther, 1959, p. 72). Conversely there was a concern that too many children were leaving grammar school prematurely (14.5 per cent of boys in 1949) clearly misallocated to an inappropriately academic education. There was too much misallocation of talent, too many factors obstructing the flow of ability while social origins still had too much influence on educational prospects. But the implications for the economy were that the education selection system was wasting ability and this was a deficiency at the heart of the country's labour formation.

The waste and misallocation of talent was intended to be eradicated by the superseding of the tripartite system and the 11-plus by the comprehensive school. Here all capabilities, academic, technical or indeed low abilities were to be catered for in the same school. This change rapidly took place from 1965 as the number of pupils in comprehensives overtook those in grammar schools from 1969 and those in modern schools from 1972 (Simon, 1991 p. 583). Yet in spite of the achievements of the comprehensives over the subsequent years they have still left us with serious lags. In 1996 12 per cent of school leavers left without reaching level 3 of the national curriculum in English and fourteen per cent in mathematics. Our international position was also low. At the Third International Mathematics and Science Study in 1995 the performance of English and Scottish students aged about 14 was below average for forty countries and significantly below the top nineteen countries, 'one could conclude that the English (and Scottish) students performed less well than might have been hoped for' (Robinson, 1997). It is also plain that an individual's employment prospects are harmed by lack of literacy and numeracy. Conversely employers are not satisfied with the output of the school system, 18 per cent finding that there is a skills gap between what they require in employees and what they find in youngsters they recruit from school (Robinson, 1997 p. 32). Yet Peter Robinson urges us not to exaggerate these defects, only 4 per cent of employers were concerned about defects in literacy and numeracy, there seems to be little correlation internationally between mathematical attainment and per capita GNP and some of the most successful Asian economies – Hong Kong and Singapore – have high illiteracy rates. Yet for the former 'workshop of the world' to be in the lower half of a long league table of forty countries in mathematics in the 1990s gives pause for thought, especially in the light of Sandberg's historical finding that educational levels more often predict future than reflect contemporary economic strengths.

The transition to comprehensive schools might not have been necessary had the 1944 Act been implemented with a genuine tripartite structure. The Act did not require this but the explanatory pamphlets sent out by the new Ministry of Education to LEAs assumed that the tripartite forms would be followed. But the defects of selection for the grammar school were compounded by the neglect of the new secondary technical school. In practice the balance of the system as it developed was in the curious ratio of 1 secondary technical school pupil to 7 grammar school pupils to 17 secondary modern school pupils. Some 25 per cent of primary school pupils went to grammar schools as 11-plus 'passes' but most of the rest, some 70 per cent, went as 'failures' to secondary modern schools. The idea of running an education system in which 70 per cent of the population are classified as failures at the age of eleven is rather bizarre. Most bizarre is the fact that the failures included the present Archbishop of Canterbury, Dr George Carey. Ideally there should have been an intermediate position with a testing of mechanical aptitude and an allocation of youngsters with such talent to the STSs in at least the same proportion as the academically inclined went to the grammar school. But only about 4 per cent of children went to STSs which declined from a peak of 324 in 1946 down to 184 by 1964.

Why was there this neglect and decline? We have seen reasons for the lack of development of these schools in the inter-war years. To these were added others of the post-war period. Labour ministers of the 1940s saw the grammar school as the ladder of advancement for the children of their working-class supporters and some of the old Left suspicion of the technical education of children was retained. Conservative local authorities also preferred grammar schools as the pathway to middle-class professions which their supporters desired for their own offspring to replicate their own status, especially if they were unable or unwilling to afford public schools. Very few MPs had any first hand experience of JTSs or STSs as part of their own schooling – never as many as 1 per cent in the period 1951–66. The psychologists remained sceptical. Sir Cyril Burt, the recently knighted doyen of educational psychology held firmly to his view that it was quite impossible to determine at the age of eleven (the new age of entry to the Secondary Technical School) whether a child had technical and mechanical aptitudes, although it was possible to measure general intelligence. These considerations weighed heavily with Chief Education Officers who saw STSs as high-cost schools with no valid mode of selection, and preferred to have nothing to do with them. There was also the problem created by the confusion over the purposes of the secondary modern school. The secondary modern took 70 per cent of children and yet little thought was given to its purpose and content. Accordingly it tended to justify itself by moving into craft and technical teaching. This unfortunately confirmed the suggestion that technical subjects were inferior ones only appropriate for academic failures. Indeed for lack of other selection criteria academic failure was taken as a proxy for technical aptitude. The taking up of technical subjects by secondary modern schools also suggested that there was no need for a specific stream of secondary technical schools if the secondary moderns could overlap their activities cheaply.

But the STSs were finally wrecked by two factors – the Conservative policies of Sir David Eccles and the Labour policies in favour of comprehensive schools (Sanderson, 1994). In 1955 David Eccles as Minister of Education decided not to sanction any further STSs on the grounds that technical ability was undetectable at eleven, that in any case academically able children who began to manifest such abilities should develop them in grammar schools in conjunction with scientific studies. Those with less ability could be catered for in secondary modern schools where crafts were available. The STSs were seen as 'aptitude' schools and anomalous alongside grammar and secondary modern schools, entry to which was determined by 'ability'. Eccles would have none of them and Edward Boyle the other leading Conservative Minister of the time was equally hostile to the STS. Many STSs gradually merged into bilateral grammar-technical schools, then the rise of comprehensive schools swallowed up the tripartite system. Between 1965 and 1975 the proportions of children in comprehensive schools rose from 8.5 per cent to 64.3 per cent and those in STSs fell from 3 per cent to 0.5 per cent. Labour sought to sweep away all the problems arising from the unfairnesses of grammar school selection and the low status and unclear function of the secondary moderns by replacing both with comprehensive schools. Yet in doing so they completed the destruction of the technical school sector. The deliberate neglect and demise of the STS was one of the most harmful educational developments of the post-war years. It lay at the heart of many of the difficulties in the formation of an effective labour force in other areas.

The loss of the JTS/STS sector might in turn have been less damaging if the existing school system had been more effective in receiving technology into the curriculum. The problem was that the prestige of the grammar school was associated with the prestige of pure science. The O-level science curriculum was overloaded, too abstract and disregarding of the relevance of science for industry. The Science Masters' Association which might have influenced matters was too closely identified with grammar and public schools. As the STSs were dying in the 1960s two divergent approaches emerged. The Nuffield Foundation Science Teaching Project began in 1962 but was chiefly concerned to promote pure academic science for the ablest pupils to the neglect of applied science, technology and engineering. This was perpetuating the superior image of pure science and the lower status of technology and engineering. In 1965 the Schools Council Project in Technology took a different tack emphasising practical crafts. Relations between the Nuffield project and the Schools Council project were discordant with the DES remaining aloof. In consequence the urgent interest in technology in the mid 1960s dwindled as 'conflicting attitudes and interests of those groups involved in this field generated tensions which weakened reforming initiatives' and in consequence 'despite major efforts there has been no technological revolution in the schools' (McCulloch, Jenkins and Layton, 1985 pp. 184, 207).

The attempt to introduce technology into the schools through the National Curriculum fared little better. Following the Education Act of 1988 Design and Technology became part of the national curriculum in 1990. Yet a follow-up report found that 'technology in the national curriculum is a mess'. The emphasis on making and doing had become more diffused as more and more linkages of technology with arts, crafts, business studies, IT, home economics were required so 'from being essentially about designing and making it had become generalised problem solving without a specific knowledge base' (Smithers and Robinson, 1992). Instead of actually making a desk-tidy pupils were required to write about how they would have approached the task – the task itself remaining unperformed. The literary and academic again dominated over the manual and practical. Smithers and Robinson called urgently for a refocusing of the subject of technology as one clearly defined as 'concerned with the design and manufacture of products and systems' with a properly qualified staff and workshop practices – just as the old JTS had done.

The failure of technology in schools has led to a plethora of schemes (and acronyms) partly a consequence of James Callaghan's speech at Ruskin College in October 1976 calling for education and training to make a greater contribution to economic performance. In 1978 the Youth Opportunities Programme (YOP) was started to give unemployed school leavers work experience through tuition and practical work studies. Employers welcomed it as cheap labour but this was only short training which Aldcroft regards 'had very little merit' (Aldcroft, 1992). In 1983 this was replaced by the Youth Training Scheme (YTS). At this time a quarter of sixteen and seventeen-year-olds not in full-time education were unemployed. The Youth Training Scheme provided a subsidy to employees and absorbed unemployment by training some 400,000 a year by the late 1980s. Although it was intended as the most significant development in training since the 1964 Industrial Training Act yet it was accounted a failure. Most trainees were in administrative, clerical and retail work with only 13 per cent in engineering and what could be regarded as manufacturing industry. Moreover the one-year 'course' was too short for the acquiring of proper craft and technician skills and, most damningly, less than a quarter of YTS trainees left with any qualifications at all (Jones, 1988). Aldcroft dismisses it as 'little short of a disaster' (Aldcroft, 1992).

The YTS in turn was replaced by Youth Training (YT) in 1990 – itself too loose and unstructured – covering only 2 per cent of the labour market and more a means of disguising unemployment than providing effective training. There was another layer of initiatives dealing with adults. In 1972 the Training Opportunities Scheme (TOPS) provided short courses for unemployed adults but it lacked skill depth; it was replaced by Employment Training (ET), which was itself of low quality. At the school level, Technical and Vocational Education Initiative (TVEI) was started in 1983, providing funds for projects in schools in technology, IT, catering and horticulture but although offering a diploma it was not a curriculum or a qualification. In 1985 the Certificate of Pre-Vocational Education (CPVE) was introduced, a one-year programme of work-related subjects for students staying on in further education but not preparing for A-levels. In 1986 the National Council for Vocational Qualifications (NCVQ) was set up to rationalise and evaluate the multitude of courses and qualifications and in 1990 Training and Enterprise Councils were established as employer-led bodies to assess local training needs and assume responsibility for ensuring that they were met. In spite of this plethora of initiatives 'no comprehensive and coherent programme of training of good quality' was created (Aldcroft, 1992) and Finegold and Soskice dismiss them, as 'an unco-ordinated series of reforms' (Finegold and Soskice, 1988).

The situation has been exacerbated by the decline of apprenticeship from the 1960s. Although there was much talk of a decline in the 1900s yet apprenticeship remained remarkably robust in England until after World War II. But the decline has since been genuine with a fall in number from 389,000 apprentices and trainees in 1964 to 87,000 by 1990 (Gospel, 1993a p. 19). Various criticisms were levelled at the old apprenticeship system. It was restricted primarily to young males in a limited range of trades. Its criteria were more concerned with the serving of time (usually five or three years rather than the original seven) than the attainment of standards. It was accused of being too narrow to respond to the changing needs of industry and it perpetuated demarcations between trades and craft restrictions (Gospel, 1993b).

Several factors lie behind the recent decline of apprenticeship since the 1960s. Firstly, the increasing numbers staying on at school because of the raising of the school-leaving age, the expansion of sixth forms and especially of higher education have all diverted young people from the apprenticeship track. One might say educational experience has broadened. Yet it is questionable whether many mediocre arts graduates swept up in the university expansion and with low job expectations would not have been better acquiring craft skills as a path to self employment. Secondly, technical change has eradicated many of the trade jobs to which apprenticeship led. This is evident in printing and in some forms of engineering. Yet technical change and apprenticeship have not proved incompatible in Germany, where new occupations are linked to apprenticeship. Thirdly, the decline in trade union power especially in the 1980s undermined the apprenticeship system. Unions had been strong supporters of apprenticeship, since it was a means of regulating entry into craft trades and hence maintaining the high differential of craftsmens wages: 'trade unions have provided an important institutional support for the apprenticeship system and the reduction in union power may have contributed to the decline of the system' (Gospel, 1993a p. 12). Fourthly, changes in wages and employment have militated against apprenticeship. The higher wages of apprentices in relation to those of craftsmen contributed to the reluctance of employers to take on apprentices. Moreover higher levels of unemployment from the 1970s, even of skilled men, reduced the urgency for employers to shoulder the burden of training when craftsmen could be recruited in the open market. By the 1980s employers in Japan, West Germany and the United States devoted 3 per cent of their annual turnover to training, whereas in Britain it was only 0.14 per cent (Rose, 1994 p. 339).

Perhaps most important in undermining apprenticeship, however, has been a series of government initiatives. In the context of unease about apprenticeship in the 1960s the 1964 Industrial Training Act created the Industrial Training Boards. These had the power to levy charges on firms, increased training on the job and more apprentices acquired formal qualifications thereby. However, change was to follow. The YTS and YT were two-year training schemes with funds provided by the government. The young people were not apprentices but trainees with government grants, there was a dearth of good training places, employers were not obliged to participate, much of the training was at a low level and more related to reducing unemployment. Some employers upgraded some YT trainees to apprenticeships but worst of all, others replaced their apprenticeship programmes with YT. Further upheaval followed as the Thatcher government repealed the Industrial Training Act and abolished most of the ITBs replacing them with TECs. Howard Gospel is scathing on what has emerged: 'This set of policy initiatives through the 1980s were in no way designed to support the traditional apprenticeship system. Indeed cumulatively they probably served to undermine it. Thus Britain has moved towards a very mixed and uncertain system of youth training and skill formation; deteriorating occupational labour market training; a shift towards unregulated market based provision; a simultaneous attempt to develop interfirm provision through the TEC's ... more vocationalism within schools but without a real system of school based training.' All this provided 'a very mixed system of industrial training, the effectiveness of which is uncertain' (Gospel, 1993a pp. 8, 15).

The decline in work-based apprenticeship has seen a corresponding attempt to create more academic programmes. Of the Youth Cohort, the proportion in apprenticeship fell from 13 to 9 per cent between 1989 and 1992 whereas those in full-time education doubled from 15 to 30 per cent between 1984 and 1993. Since 1993 the predominant form of full-time vocational education has been the General National Vocational Qualification (GNVQ) which began in that year and this too has been subject to searching criticism (Wolf, 1997). Firstly, three-quarters of GNVQ students are in the 'big four' subjects – tourism, health and social care, art and design, business. It is heavily weighted towards professional and service activity and there is very little science and technology. The 1997 Wolf Report deplored 'how few are entering scientific and technological disciplines'; well under 10 per cent were studying science, construction or engineering. Also much of the approach of the GNVQ was too academic: 'the typical experience of a GNVQ student for most of the year is that of a rather cosy classroom-based programme ... where material supplied by teachers (many with no vocational background) is supplemented by library visits'. Thirdly, this academic bias was increasingly consistent with the fact that half of GNVQ students expected to use the qualification not to enter work but for university entrance. Students with poor GCSEs and of an ability level markedly below those of A-level are encouraged to use GNVQs as an easier route to universities with modest entry requirements. It was the worst of both worlds. It was overoptimistic that they could be both a practical preparation for careers and at the same time the academic equivalent of A-levels for university entrance. The high drop-out rates at GNVQ also suggest the lower calibre of candidates. Yet again an attempt to create a curriculum and qualification for industry had failed to find a sufficient definition of focus. The GNVQ is also leading to the decline of other qualifications. The Certificate of Pre-Vocational Education has been phased out. The BTEC National Diplomas have declined sharply since 1993, overtaken by GNVQs. GNVQs themselves may be squeezed by the rapid rise of business studies A-level which has no such confusion of purpose.

It should be noted however that the lower level National Vocational Qualifications are highly occupational specific and valued. For example all John Lewis Partnership shop retailers take NVQs. But significantly NVQ students do not go on to the much more questionable GNVQs.

The best hope for revitalising industrial education for the young in recent years has been the City Technology College (CTC). But here again things have gone sadly wrong. These were announced by Kenneth Baker as Secretary of State for Education in 1986, proposing twenty pilot colleges with a curriculum strongly emphasising technological, scientific and practical work, business studies and design (Walford and Miller, 1991). They were to be for the 11 to 18 age group and run not by LEAs but by independent trusts, and to facilitate this the City Technology College Trust was established in May 1987. The schools were supposed to be built with private business money but the running costs met by per capita funding from the DES. The schools were not supposed to select academically like the grammar schools but take their pupils from a wide ability range and especially cater for the deprived youth of inner cities. The staff in technology subjects were paid on higher than union rates negotiated with the school governors. As such the CTCs were intended to side-step the LEAs, the comprehensive schools and the grammar schools with their failure to address technology teaching, and the trade unions. Especially they were to be a weapon in British manufacturing industry's fight back against the recession and foreign competition of the early 1980s.

However things did not develop. The CTCs depended for their financial support on industry but this was not forthcoming. Many major firms refused, the CBI and the Industrial Society were sceptical and out of 1800 firms approached only seven responded positively. There was little gain for firms to have their name expensively associated with merely one school in one place whose pupils would probably be largely irrelevant to their recruitment. Accordingly for lack of private industrial money the state had to intervene with £59 million from central government and £55 from LEA funds. This highlighted the criticism that such money would have been better spent on technology in schools throughout the state sector. But the worst aspect of the scheme was that only fifteen of the twenty intended schools ever materialised, a futile substitute for the 324 STSs of 1946 which had been allowed to wither away after the Eccles policies of the 1950s. Wooldridge asks pertinently, '300 Technical Schools failed to galvanise the educational system in the 1940s. Why should 20 Technology Colleges succeed in galvanising it in the 1990s?' (Wooldridge, 1990 p. 22).

Behind these failures or limited successes indicated in recent paragraphs lay two spectres. One was the 'might have been' of the abandoning of the STSs and the unsatisfactory attempts to find a substitute for them ever since. The other was the ever present comparison with our former enemies Germany and Japan and the awareness that their drawing away from us in economic competition was underpinned by evident superiorities in education. English youth was some two years behind its German counterpart in mathematical skills and the level of attainment of the lower half of German pupils was higher than the average level in England (Prais and Wagner, 1983). Likewise 79 per cent of Japanese children obtained higher scores in mathematics than the average English child while in the sciences English fourteen-year-olds were the bottom of the league of seventeen competitor countries (Finegold and Soskice, 1988 citing studies by Lynn and Postlethwaite). The key element in our weakness has been the neglect of education and training of post-school-leaving-age teenagers especially in the 1970s and 1980s. In the 1970s Britain had one of the lowest percentages of eighteen-year-olds in non higher vocational education – 5.7 per cent in 1976 compared with Germany's 51.8 per cent while France, Spain, Norway, Denmark and Switzerland all had higher, usually much higher levels than the United Kingdom. More specifically if we compare the experience of young people in Britain (1977) after they have finished compulsory education with those in Germany (1980), we find the following.

	Full time general education	Full time vocational education	Apprentice-ship	Work or un-employment
Germany 1980	25	18	50	7
Gt Britain 1977	32	10	14	44

By 1985 the percentages of 16–18 year olds in education and training were: 85 per cent in West Germany, 73 per cent in Japan, 66 per cent in France and 65 per cent in the United Kingdom if YTS is included. We are still behind in the 1990s (see table 6.3).

Table 6.3 Comparative educational performance, 1991

	1991 percentages		
	(a) 16 year olds reaching the equivalent of GCSE grades A–C	(b) Young people obtaining upper secondary school qualifications 18+	(c) Young people 16–19 in full and part time education and training
Germany	62	68	79
France	66	48	76
Japan	50	80	94
England	27	29	56

Source: Green and Steedman, (1993), pp. 7, 8, 16.

Various underlying factors can be seen as impeding our development in vocational education and training (VET) (Finegold and Soskice, 1988). Firstly there has been a political consensus, shared by the CBI, that education was a matter for the state but that training should be left to industry. It was not until the creation of the Manpower Services Commission in 1973 that the state developed an active labour market policy and the Department of Education and Science was not able to exercise control because of the decentralised system of English education. Accordingly LEAs and indeed teachers, opposed to vocationalism could nullify such policies. Firms in British industry were concentrated in areas of low skill whereas we did not perform so well in skill and innovation intensive products. Moreover firms financed themselves from retained profits rather than having links with investment banks and this prompted a certain short termism making it harder to invest in training that yields deferred benefits. Accordingly it has proved difficult to persuade the private sector of its responsibilities in this area which undermines the *laisser faire* belief that VET is a matter to be left to industry. It is also argued that enthusiasm for skill training has been diminished by the inadequacy of future returns as the differentials between skilled and unskilled labour were too low and much lower than in Germany. This was also linked with the high levels of trainee pay (Jones, 1988). All this has trapped Britain in what Finegold and Soskice term a 'low skills equilibrium' producing 'low quality goods and services'.

Leslie Hannah puts forward another factor. He agrees on the small base of skilled labour and our defects in creating on-the-job skills that vocational training offers and our 'bias to low technology, with a lower level of educational skills embodied in her exports than is typical of other western industrialised countries'. He also notes the inadequacy of leaving the problem to firms or indeed governments. He sees a root problem in the need to rebalance incentives. In the 1980s there was generous government assistance in fees and living costs for full-time university students, however economically irrelevant the studies. Yet someone with the initiative to take part-time evening studies relevant to their work got no help at all – 'state subsidies for the lucky few, together with a perverse denial of help to those willing to help themselves, create a very one-sided incentive structure which inevitably leads to a few people gaining expensive qualifications while the mass remain underqualified' (Hannah, 1987 p. 180). The over privilege of higher education and relative neglect of less academic vocational education was seen increasingly as an issue in the 1980s.

In all our concern in the 1960s to turn secondary education over to comprehensivisation and expand higher education, the most difficult problem which had been neglected was what to do about the education and training of non-academic working-class teenagers. The Germans continued their long tradition of Trade Continuation Schools with the institutions and the social attitudes behind them. Britain had abandoned the Continuation Schools in the 1920s and the STSs in the 1950s and this had left us laggard.

The deficiencies of education have held back the economy by regularly leading to skill shortages in times of rapid growth. The proportion of companies expecting shortages of skilled labour has risen from 2 per cent in the 1970s to 2.5 per cent by 1982 and 20 per cent by 1990. In 1990 49 per cent of manufacturing companies had problems in recruiting staff (Wooldridge, 1990). The problem is especially acute in the computing skills needed by retailers, financial services and public sector organisations. But the problem is also evident in more traditional areas. The numbers qualifying as mechnical fitters, electricians and building craftsmen was only a half to a third of the corresponding number in Germany; by 1990 two-thirds of firms in the Building Employers' Confederation reported difficulties in recruiting carpenters and bricklayers (Cassells, 1990). The skill shortages caused by educational defects create inflationary pressures as firms seek to poach this scarce resource and this in turn contributes to the widening gap of income inequality which is another peculiarly British problem.

Inequality has sharply increased since 1977 and is largely accounted for by the decline in demand for unskilled workers (Goodman, Johnson and Webb, 1997). This has been reflected in high levels of unemployment for the unskilled and the widening gap between their earnings and the higher paid. There are various reasons for this. Technical change, notably computerisation, has favoured the more skilled while the decline in employment in manufacturing from 37 per cent in 1961 to 18 per cent by 1991 and the shift to services has removed the need for machine minders and crate humpers. Most importantly, with the globalisation of trade, unskilled men are pitted in competition with even cheaper unskilled labour in developing countries. The decline in demand for unskilled labour has exceeded even its falling supply, hence the widening gap. Yet the latest IFS report sees the only solution not in redistributing income downwards from the higher earners but in raising the skill levels of the low earners through education and training. The betrayal of the non academic teenager from the spurious psychology of the 11-plus and the destruction of the STS through to the confusion of an inadequate VET lies near the heart both of economic deficiencies and social inequalities that have plagued post-war Britain.

7

Higher education and the public schools – privilege and relevance

By the end of the second world war, both the universities and the public schools remained institutions with entry restricted to a privileged few, partly by intelligence and to a large extent by wealth. In the post-war years, and especially from the 1960s, both types of institution expanded their intakes. The universities lost much of whatever sense of privilege they had in the move to mass higher education and the public schools, to a much lesser extent, increased their numbers and proportion of the school population. Yet the expansion of the universities and consequent curricular developments raised questions of how far they were becoming less relevant to the needs of an industrial society while the public schools, reviled as anti-industrial before 1914, paradoxically moved closer to the business and industrial world.

In the immediate post-war years there were demands for the expansion of the universities by the Barlow and Percy Reports and others. Although there was not yet the urgent demographic need of the 1960s the number of university students doubled from 50,002 in 1938–9 to 107,699 by 1960–1 as existing universities expanded and were joined by Nottingham, Southampton, Hull, Exeter, Leicester (upgraded from university colleges) and Keele (which was newly founded in 1949 and chartered in 1962). There were also healthy signs that the proportion of students studying science and technology rose from 25.9 per cent in 1938–9 to 40.6 per cent by 1961–2. David Edgerton who takes a sceptical view of 'decline' and the responsibility of science and education for it points out that in the 1950s this was good in comparison with European comparators, in 1954/5 Great Britain's 44 per cent of graduates studying science and technology comparing well with

West Germany's 34 per cent and France's 29. In the early 1960s Britain also compared well with competitors with 4.6 per cent of the age group 20–4 graduating in science and technology compared with 4.2 per cent in the United States, 3.2 in France and 2.2 in Germany (Edgerton, 1996 pp. 54–5). The importance attached to industrial science for military purposes in the recent war and reflecting in the greater importance attached to technology, the doubling of numbers of students and the relative decline in medical education had given higher education a healthy complexion in the 1940s and 1950s in spite of the still tiny proportion of young people going into university. It gives pause to generalised views that all of British education was defective or backward and an inevitable contributor to decline at this time.

The expansion of the new universities in the 1960s might have been an opportunity to gear higher education yet more closely to the economy, as had been the case in the 1880s with the rise of the civic universities. The reasons for the expansion were largely couched in social terms, the response to demography and demands for equality of opportunity. The birth rate rose at the end of the War such that eighteen-year-olds were to increase from 533,000 in 1959 to a peak of 812,000 by 1965. Moreover there was already a trend towards staying on in the sixth form from 32,000 to 53,000 between 1947 and 1958 among children born in the low and declining birth-rate years of the 1930s. If the increasing tendency to enter sixth forms was to be continued by the bulge generation then, without expansion, the universities would be 25,000 places short by 1967. It was also hoped that expanded universities would reduce the differences in the chances of going to university between social classes. Of children of higher professional parents born in the late 1930s $14\frac{1}{2}$ per cent went to universities but only $\frac{1}{2}$ per cent of semi- and unskilled workers did so (Little and Westergaard, 1964). Robbins thought that the gap for all degree-level higher education was even greater – a third in comparison with 1 per cent (Robbins, 1963 p. 50).

Alongside the social reasons there were also those that took account of the needs of the economy. Michael Kaser showed the close relationship between annual growth rates of GNP and numbers of university students per 1,000 primary students in the 1950s. At the top of the league tables were the fast growers, Japan with 7 per cent growth and 48 students, Germany with 11 per cent and 41 while at the bottom were England and Wales with 2 per cent and 20 respectively (Kaser, 1966). Kaser was careful to point out that economic growth could as much be a cause as a consequence of a high or low ranking in higher education provision, but the assumptions of the time were that expanding higher education could improve the economy. Robbins had recognised the needs of industry by calling for an increase in the proportion of technology degrees compared with those in pure science. But he himself was cautious over what the links between university expansion and economic improvement might be. As an economist he was sceptical about measuring future manpower needs, the rate of return on educational investment or the relation between the amount of education and industrial productivity. He took a low commonsense view that there must be some benefits to the economy from expanding the universities.

However the new universities were not created in response to the Robbins Report. They were already being planned from 1958 and some were the outcomes of movements going back to just before the First World War. Sussex, Essex, York and East Anglia had already opened before the Robbins Report was published. The new universities were the product of the then UGC and its chairman Sir Keith Murray and there were several features of the UGC-Murray influence which disengaged the new creations of the sixties from direct service to the economy. They were usually located in ancient cities – three of them (Colchester, Lancaster, Norwich) with charters coincidentally dating from the five years from 1189 to 1194. Indeed they were known to the UGC as the 'Shakespeareans' the names of their cities resonant of the titles of aristocratic characters in Shakespeare history plays. With the exception of Warwick they were more usually in cathedral cities notable for architecture and culture rather than industry. Also the UGC insisted on minimal 200-acre sites which meant that the universities had to be rural campuses in the countryside outside even the cities from which they took their names. Furthermore Murray also insisted that the new institutions should not grow out of existing Victorian technical institutions in their cities and connection with them was discouraged. This was to assert the independence and totally fresh start of the new universities.

Finally the UGC guided the Academic Planning Boards away from thinking of expensive vocational courses of industrial or professional application. Instead fast growth was to be achieved in the traditional liberal arts, the then fashionable social sciences and the normal theoretical natural sciences. Innovation was to be in interdisciplinary combinations within broad subject areas rather than in specialisms sharply geared to local industry as had been the Victorian civic university strategy. Accordingly there was some dissonance between the rhetoric calling for university expansion to vitalise the economy and the real nature of the universities created. Sussex, UEA, and Kent had no significant connections with industry in the sixties. Essex was allowed the engineering denied to Norwich while Lancaster began its strong business studies. Warwick was the most industrially engaged of the new universities with engineering and management relating to the automobile and electrical industries. Warwick was quite the most successful of the new universities in raising money then and arguably the most successful of the new sixties universities since. Yet overall it is fair to say that the new universities were not especially committed to industry and much of what involvement there was lay in management and economics rather than applied science and technology. In this there was a sharp contrast with the civic universities of Victorian times. A sympathetic but shrewd observer of the time noted that 'it is a paradox that whereas the talk of politicians was of the need for technologists and applied scientists, the new universities devoted so much of their resources to the arts and social sciences' (Beloff, 1968). One might now go further and argue that in the sixties, the very decade when Britain's economic falling behind was becoming most marked, there was a missed opportunity in the direction taken by the new university expansion.

This was not evident at the time because however disengaged the 'Shakespeareans' were from industry it was thought that this would be compensated for by the parallel development of the technological universities. In 1956 several leading technical colleges usually of Victorian origin were designated as Colleges of Advanced Technology. They were to concentrate on advanced work and degrees. In 1962 these CATs received direct grants from the Ministry of Education and then in 1965 were elevated to university status with university charters and financed by the UGC. Eight of them were in England – Battersea (the University of Surrey), Aston, Bradford, Bath, Brunel, Loughborough, Salford and Northampton (City University) were separately chartered while Chelsea became part of the University of London. In Scotland Heriot Watt became a separate university in Edinburgh while the Royal College of Science and Technology in Glasgow had already become the University of Strathclyde in 1964.

As the CATs moved on to become universities so in 1966 a further group of leading technical colleges, initally twenty-seven and ultimately thirty were designated as Polytechnics, likewise to concentrate on advanced work and prepare students for degrees through the University of London and the National Council for Academic Awards which had been established in 1964. These Polytechnics remained under local authority control. This was the 'binary system' with part of higher education under the UGC and part still in the LEA sector. Here was a galaxy of institutions long devoted to science and technology to offset the arts–social studies emphasis of the new campuses. It was hoped that this would meet Robbins' demands for more technology and especially more technology in proportion to the pure sciences. The reclassification of what was included as a 'university' resulted in an increase of students studying applied science from 15.2 per cent in 1961/2 to 20.6 per cent by 1966/7. Also the proportion of first-degree graduates taking up employment in industry and commerce rose steadily from 56.4 per cent in 1962 to 66 per cent by 1969.

However things began to go wrong. Symbolically the technological universities began to drop 'technology' from their titles. Also they were not attracting students. In 1969 more than 1,500 university places remained unfilled mostly in science and engineering. Partly this was attributed to the poor image of technology in schools. There were also more precise reasons. Firstly there was the Dainton 'swing' identified in reports by Sir Frederick Dainton in 1966 and 1968. This showed that there had been a steady increase in the proportions of students taking A-levels in mathematics and science up to a peak of 64.5 per cent by 1960, yet thereafter there was a falling away and a sharp swing towards the arts and especially to the then fashionable social studies. Secondly, this in turn was partly the result of a decline in real wages of teachers which had been allowed to take place in the 1950s. Schoolmasters who had entered what they regarded as a profession in the good times of the 1930s and returned, perhaps idealistically, after the War found themselves betrayed. Any scientist or mathematician of ability was ill – advised to become a schoolteacher in the 1950s and the quality of science teaching and especially mathematics deteriorated. The situation has hardly been rectified. Wooldridge deplores in 1990 that 'science graduates either refuse to enter the teaching profession or leave it as soon as they can. In 1985 not one Cambridge physics graduate chose school teaching as a career. In 1986 a quarter of mathematics teachers and a third of physics teachers lacked appropriate qualifications' (Wooldridge, 1990). A vicious circle was set up – constant public pay restraint deters science graduates of quality from entering teaching in rational preference for industry and business, poor teaching deters school children from studying science and constrains the potential supply of applicants for science degrees and hence science graduates. Thirdly the problems of technological universities were compounded at an early stage in that their grants were cut 1968/9–1971/2 for failure to meet intake targets whereas arts oriented universities determined on expansion were further rewarded. In this way the subject preferences of sixth formers were allowed to determine government policy whether it was in the national interest or not. Expansion for increasing participation ratios was taking precedence over the technological needs of industry (Sanderson, 1991).

At root were the problems we referred to earlier – the elimination of the STS and the failure of other sorts of school to cater for applied sciences. The grammar schools were too academic and preferred science, secondary moderns were not supposed to take pupils intelligent enough to study science and technology at university and the comprehensives did not have the funds or equipment the old STSs had possessed through their links with the technical colleges. In the 1930s Lord Percy had envisaged a dual track of grammar schools leading to universities and secondary technical schools leading to technological universities. But the policies of the 1950s had destroyed the technical school part of this link and the attempt to create a layer of technological universities as part of the higher education expansion of the 1960s was distorted and stifled thereby.

Table 7.1 Proposed and actual subject spread of technological universities, 1963, 1974

	Recommended by principals of CATS to Robbins	Actual spread 1974
Technology	65	43
Science	15	24.6
Social science	10	19.6
Arts	10	12.8

Source: Venables (1978), p. 295.

This in turn had unfortunate effects. The technological universities and polytechnics unable to compete with civic universities in applied science and unsupported from below by a school system that was failing to produce potential technologists adopted a new strategy. They began to compete with the 'Shakespearean' universities in seeking to attract increasing numbers of arts and social studies sixth formers. They began a process of 'policy drift' of reducing their commitment to their noble Victorian roots in science and technology and adopted the view that 'proper' universities had a greater balance of arts and sciences. They backtracked on what they had told Robbins they intended to do in 1963 and moved more strongly to pure science, arts and social studies (Venables, 1978) and so it was also with the Polytechnics which became universities in the 1990s. But by the end of the 1970s over half their students were already in arts and social studies subjects (Sanderson, 1991 p. 176). Indeed in the 1970s a sample of ten universities and ten polytechnics showed that whereas 41.5 per cent of the universities' publications were in arts and 58.5 per cent were in sciences the corresponding figures for the polytechnics were 42.2 for arts and 57.8 per cent in sciences. The polytechnics had a higher, not a lower proportionate output than the universities in arts publications (Locke, 1989 p. 186). It was as if they realised that they could not create a genuine alternative tradition of technical higher education as France and Germany had had through long tradition in their *grandes écoles* and THs. They saw their only way forward as a convergence on the orthodox liberal education ideal. But we ended up in the 1990s with an overextended and unaffordable system of higher education with too many institutions costing far more per student than European competitors and even the United States and Japan and absorbing four times the resources of primary and secondary education – a proportion again far in excess of any other advanced country (National Commission for Education, 1995 p. 44). This lies behind the severe squeeze on the 'unit of resource' which the universities are experiencing in the 1990s with the consequent paradox of the closing of some science and engineering departments which might have been useful to industry.

The higher education system has had particular difficulty in producing two leading types of labour for the economy, the higher educated engineer and the manager. Albu points to the low proportion of engineers in the metal manufacturing industries, in the United Kingdom a mere 1.8 per cent compared with 5–6 per cent in France and Germany in the 1970s. Professional engineers also had lower wage differentials against blue-collar workers in Britain than in France and Germany (Albu, 1980) and sixth formers studying A level mathematics (and thinking of future careers) accorded a very low status to engineering, ranking mechanical engineering only eighteenth out of twenty-two occupations in order of prestige. Underuse, underpay and low prestige bode ill for the position of the engineer in manufacturing industry.

There were also serious confusions about what engineering education should consist of, mirroring confusions about 'technology' in the school curriculum. Divall has shown that between the 1890s and 1930s there was a consensus between universities and employers on the balance between theoretical science and practical work experience in the formation of the engineer. However in the late 1930s a small group of influential engineers wanted to make university engineering a more sophisticated scientific and theoretical subject. This would give engineering more of the prestige associated with medicine and the pure sciences, distinguish the universities more from the technical colleges and emphasise innovative research as a function of engineering education rather than the transmission of the details of current practice. This new view was embodied in the 1940s and 1950s in the approach at Cambridge, the largest engineering school in Britain. This seemed acceptable to employers who used graduates for research. In the 1960s the tide swung again and criticisms arose that the over-scientific education of engineers had produced graduates unable to apply their knowledge to the detail of design and insufficiently concerned with the finished product. The lack of unanimity among senior engineers and employers left universities confused as to what they should be producing – highly scientific professional engineers or men less schooled in theoretical science but introduced more to practical design and even broader management skills. This confusion was accompanied by a sharp decline in interest among school leavers in studying university engineering of any kind in the 1960s and at the other end, employers gave no indication through salary rewards that they valued one sort of engineer or another. Divall concludes that the wish of the universities to train graduates in skills needed by British industry 'was not matched by a similar desire among employers in the engineering industry' (Divall, 1991).

If there were problems with the professional education of engineers so there was with managers (Aldcroft, 1995). In the mid 1950s it was found that the most favoured qualifications for managers were attendance at a major public school and an arts degree from Oxford or Cambridge which took precedence over scientific and technical qualifications. In the immediate post-war years only about 10 per cent of managers were graduates and fewer than half of directors in charge of production had any qualifications in engineering or science. By the 1970s and 1980s although the position in Britain was improving it was much behind that of our foreign competitors. In the early 1970s fewer than half of top executives in large British firms were university graduates compared with 60–90 per cent in Germany, France, Sweden, Belgium, and the United States. In 1987 Charles Handy found similarly that 24 per cent of leading British managers had degrees compared with 62–65 per cent in France and Germany and 85 per cent in the United States and Japan. Still as late as 1990 less than a quarter of company directors had professional or managerial qualifications (Keeble, 1992, p. 162). Aldcroft is blunt, 'no other country has neglected its managerial stock to the extent that Britain has done' (Aldcroft, 1995 p. 109).

Awareness of this led to some action. The Robbins and Franks Reports in 1963 urged greater attention to management education leading to two postgraduate schools being set up in London and Manchester. Universities then jumped on the bandwagon with over one hundred offering management degrees by the late 1980s but these were, in Aldcroft's view, 'often run on a shoe string with inadequate staffing ... not all of whom were properly qualified to fill the task in hand'. Indeed it is difficult to see why a successful professional manager should transfer to the relatively low pay and status work of university teaching. Keeble finds that the enthusiasm for management education in the 1960s was not sustained and that management education 'had not yet provided for the nation a well educated and trained industrial management' (Keeble, 1992 p. 158).

Robert Locke, with considerable American and European experience, finds several defects in British management education since the War (Locke, 1989). It was unfortunate that although Operational Research was pioneered in Britain during the War yet in peacetime this developed in American but not in British universities. There was a similar backwardness in linear programming in economics. This was more developed in engineering but there was not that interchange of economics and engineering studies which good management courses would have brought about. Although business schools were created yet Locke thinks that by international standards the results 'have disappointed'. Only forty-one of the leading one hundred firms have given any substantial financial support to business schools. There is also a difference of view about the MBA which is so important in the United States. The British academic view prefers a two-year course but most industrialists favour only one year and regard the extra year as a waste of time. British employers also do not regard it desirable to move from the first degree to the MBA as is the case in the United States. Moreover business studies had a low status and appeal at the first degree level. It was not until 1980 that it appeared in the top twenty of the most popular degrees and then at number seventeen – compared with Germany where it is the second most popular after Law. To an expert outside observer like Locke the difficulties over management education in Britain and its low status 'demonstrates how certain features of British education persistently shape university education, i.e. the humanistic–science emphasis and the weakness of economically purposeful education' (Locke, 1989 pp. 190–1).

If there is fair unanimity about the defects of non-academic teenagers, university, engineering and management education there is a divergence of view about the contentious area of the public schools. There is continued criticism that the public schools perpetuate the same élites and buy privilege with money. Some critics see this as damaging to the economy. Will Hutton in an influential commentary considers that 'the country denies itself access to some of the best scientific and artistic talent by organising education in such an inequitable manner' and by devaluing vocational training (Hutton, 1995 pp. 214–15). Interestingly Correlli Barnett, so critical of public schools in the 1860–1940 period, does not carry his strictures into the post-war years and this reflects an important change. For it can be argued, contrary to Hutton, that the public schools changed from being either irrelevant to or a malign drag on the economy to being institutions highly appropriate for businessmen.

Ian Weinberg studying fifteen public schools in the sixties found that 'businessmen comprised the largest group of parents'. Conversely by the late fifties a consistent 46–53 per cent of the output of all public schools were entering careers in industry and commerce (Weinberg, 1967 pp. 161, 149) and 57 per cent of existing businessmen were ex-public school boys (Rubinstein, 1986). The 1944 Act by abolishing fee-paying in state schools removed the possibility of 11-plus failures from business backgrounds merely going to the local grammar school as fee payers. The abolition of the direct grant grammar schools in 1975 closed a further loophole. The resort to the independent sector was the only alternative. Also after the failure of schemes to provide subsidised places for poor children at the public schools the schools themselves became ever more entrepreneurial and prosperous, raising fees, improving facilities and appealing to the wealthy. Old parental clients in declining professions such as teaching and the Church fell away to be replaced by those with business money. Moreover the schools themselves became more attractive to this class. In 1955 business firms established the Industrial Fund for the Advancement of Scientific Education in schools and by 1957 141 companies including Shell, ICI, and Courtaulds had contributed over £3 million for public school science laboratories to encourage future public schools scientists and engineers for industry. By 1956 a half of public school sixth formers were mathematics and science specialists and boys studying science had trebled since the mid-thirties. 'Parents were interested in science and the schools wanted to adapt to business organisations' need for scientifically educated personnel' (Weinberg, 1967 p. 72). A further consequence was that science facilities in public schools became much superior to those in grammar schools. The expectation that public schools would fade into irrelevance as grammar schools matched their quality receded. Threats, though unfulfilled, to abolish the public schools or integrate them into the state system forced on what has been termed the public schools' revolution (Rae, 1981). John Rae, the former headmaster of Westminster, has characterised these changes. There was a continued swing to science, 'the time British public school boys once spent writing Latin verses is now spent writing computer programmes' and half of the public schoolboys going to university in 1980 would be studying engineering, science and medicine (Rae, 1981 p. 160).

The schools themselves became more commercially minded, quadrupling their average fees between 1966 and 1980 and setting up various public relations and marketing organisations in the 1970s. Pupils accordingly rose from 4 per cent of schoolboys in the pre-war years to 7 per cent in the post-war years. The attitude of parents changed, becoming less concerned about the schools producing 'gentlemen' but now seeking value for money in academic results for their children which could be converted into lucrative careers as a return on an expensive but high yielding investment. Schools themselves became less concerned about 'blues' among their staff and more about first-class and PhD degrees. This paid off, as by 1979 independent schools were winning 64 per cent of open awards to Oxford and Cambridge and although public schools teach only 6 or 7 per cent of British children yet they win a quarter of all A-level passes and a half of all grade A passes (Wooldridge, 1990 p. 17). This had a consequent effects on careers. By 1977 engineering was the single most popular career for public schoolboys (Rae, 1981 p. 161). As the Empire, Church and armed services declined or contracted and the public service and education became much less attractive careers, so industry and business became commensurately more so. The public schools have continued to improve their quality and assert their advantages over the state schools by the reduction in their pupil/teacher ratios from 13 in 1980/1 to 10 by 1994/5 while the state ratio has remained a fairly constant 1 to 19 (Szreter, 1997 p. 99). Whatever the defects of other parts of the education and training system, the public school revolution was a notable success, the schools – businesses themselves – reacting flexibly to market opportunity and political threat. Would that the universities had been able to follow a similar path.

Yet the grounds for criticism of contemporary public schools have shifted from those which applied before 1914. Modern critics admit the quality of the schools but see them as symptomatic of a society that sees education as a private privileged good to be competed for rather than as a serious investment in national economic competitiveness. Moreover, by producing a high proportion of the future leaders of society they perpetuate this attitude of which the differential pupil/teacher ratios are an indicator. The public schools, for some, represent a precedence of libertarian individualism over a concern for national education as a component in economic performance (Szreter, 1997).

Conclusion

Various common themes recur over this long sweep of time. Firstly there is the persistent strength of the belief in liberal education with its emphasis on gentlemanly values and the cultivation of the mind for its own sake. There is nothing wrong with this except the second-rate status which it conferred on vocational, practical, technical and commercial training for earning a living. It lay behind the Victorian preference for the ancient universities over the civics and the preference even for Oxford over the then superior Cambridge before 1914. This in turn shaped many of the attitudes and curricula of the public schools. We see it in the slow growth of the JTSs and the eventual demise of the Secondary Technical Schools under the preference of parents and politicians for the grammar school. Some see it in Morant's suspicion of technical grammar schools. It is still reflected in the recurrent complaints of British engineers that they are undervalued. More recently it shaped the formation of the new universities in the 1960s and the forsaking of their noble Victorian technical roots by many of the technological and polytechnic universities as they converged on the old liberal arts ideal. Ironically these liberal arts subjects, anxious of their 'uselessness' now seek to justify their value – with varying degrees of credibility – in terms of 'embedded transferable skills' of potential use to employers. We were unusual in abandoning the stream of technical education for schoolgoing teenagers just as our inability to accept and understand the prestige and specialism of the French *grande école* and German TH sets us culturally apart.

Second whatever the defects of education there is ample long-term evidence of the apathy of employers towards education and training. We have seen Victorian complaints to this effect, of their indifference to the college-trained man whether from civic university or municipal 'tech'. The old preference for apprenticeship is understandable but it held back technical education in the interwar years with its perpetuation of the 'after tea' training culture. They were broadly indifferent to the JTSs and STSs and did nothing to save the latter. The Industrial Training Act of 1964 tried to force them into training and they welcomed its demise. The expectations that employers would back the City Technology Colleges were disappointed. The plethora of unsatisfactory VET schemes since 1976 suggests a failure of employers themselves to get a grip on the system to help create something of a stable nature with solid standards acceptable to themselves. For lack of this they are left recurrently to complain of skill shortages and unsatisfactory recruits. It is seen most recently at a higher level in the very tardy development of management education in Britain compared with most major competitors. Throughout this time education has been confused by a plethora of conflicting advice from employers concerning what they required ranging from the vocationally very specific to the broadly irrelevant which has not helped educators decide what they should be doing (Silver, 1983).

Thirdly for most of this period the education system has provided only a constricted access to high ability. We have seen it eased with Morant's creation of the municipal grammar school and the expanding scholarship system both into schools and from them into universities. Then the evolution of secondary education for all from the inter-war years and through the Butler Act and subsequently with comprehensivisation broadened the system. Yet access to education was very largely dependent on social class for most of this period with all the wastage and misallocation of talent that that implied. What was a matter of angst in the 1950s and 1960s had been accepted as normal hitherto and the consequent lack of flow of ability into industry – often masked by high unemployment – has been a long-term inhibitor of the raising of the standards of the labour force.

Yet we need not be too pessimistic. There are good signs for the future. In 1997 Britain rose in the World Competitiveness Index from nineteenth to eleventh, overtaking Germany, there are recent proposals for schemes for Life Long Learning and a University of

Industry and a New Deal whereby employers are encouraged to train unemployed youth. Measures introduced in the 1980s to require a national curriculum, raise standards in schools and universities through league tables, and rigorous inspection and quality assessment systems seem to be working. Knighthoods and DBEs for headteachers in 1998 and proposals for highly paid classroom teachers express a concern to raise the status of the teaching profession. The charging of fees in universities may release resources especially since in the 1990s taking a degree still yields a 7 per cent annual rate of return through lifetime earnings (Bennett, Glennester, Nevison, 1993). A resultingly more calculating attitude by students will influence their demand for education in more vocational and career-oriented directions. Indeed many of the features of the influential report of Sir Claus Moser and others are being put into effect (National Commission on Education, 1995). It is also ironical to note that Japan and other Far Eastern countries held as exemplars in this regard are now suffering severe economic recessions notwithstanding their much trumpeted educational achievements.

Britain is a rich and humane country and education has undoubtedly contributed to that over the last hundred years though, as the above discussion shows, many things could have been done better. For the future, in our concern for academic excellence we must take much more care not to neglect the non academic teenager too easily rejected by the system. Nor should we be too beglamoured by the belief that all useless knowledge is mind trainingly 'liberal'. Above all we need to see the education of the people less as a kind of humane charity and social service and recognise it more as 'fundamental and essential for the promotion of economic growth' (Szreter, 1997 p. 95). The Victorians could afford these older attitudes which we, in more pressing times, can not.

Bibliography

Note: place of publication is London, unless stated otherwise.

The following are valuable surveys of this period

Simon, Brian (1965) *Education and the Labour Movement 1870–1920.*
  (1974) *The Politics of Educational Reform 1920–1940.*
  (1991) *Education and the Social Order 1940–1990.*
Lowe, Roy (1988) *Education in the Post War Years, a Social History.*
  (1997) *Schooling and Social Change 1964–1990.*

Specialist references in the text

Abbott, A. (1933) *Education for Industry and Commerce in England* (Oxford).
Ahlstrom, G. (1982) *Engineers and Industrial Growth.*
Albu, Austen (1980) 'British Attitudes to Engineering Education: A Historical Perspective' in Keith Pavitt, *Technical Innovation and British Economic Performance.*
Aldcroft, D. H.(1964) 'The Entrepreneur in the British Economy 1870–1914', *Economic History Review* 17 no 1 August.
  (1975) 'Investment and Utilisation of Manpower: Great Britain and her Rivals 1870–1914' in B. M. Ratcliffe ed., *Great Britain and her World* (Manchester).
  (1982) 'Britain's Economic Decline 1870–1980' in G. Roderick and M. Stephens, *The British Malaise* (Lewes).
  (1992) *Education, Training and Economic Performance 1944 to 1990* (Manchester).
  (1995) 'The Missing Dimension: Management Education and Training in Postwar Britain' in Derek H. Aldcroft and Anthony Slaven, eds., *Enterprise and Management, Essays in Honour of Peter L. Payne.*
Alford, B. W. E. (1988) *British Economic Performance 1945–1975.*

Anderson, C. Arnold (1959) 'The Social Composition of University Student Bodies, the Recruitment of Nineteenth Century Elites in Four Nations' in *The Year Book of Education*, Section 5, Chapter 5.

Anderson, C. Arnold and Schnaper, Miriam (1952) *School and Society in England, Social Backgrounds of Oxford and Cambridge Students* (Washington).

Anderson, Eugene N. (1970) 'The Prussian Volksschule in the Nineteenth Century' in Gerhard A. Ritter, *Entstehung und Wandel der Modernen Gesellschaft* (Berlin).

Anderson R. D. (1983) *Education and Opportunity in Victorian Scotland, Schools and Universities* (Oxford).

(1992) *Universities and Elites in Britain since 1800* (Cambridge).

(1997) *Scottish Education since the Reformation* (Dundee).

Bailey, Bill (1990) 'Technical Education and Secondary Schooling 1905–1945' in Penny Summerfield and Eric Evans, *Technical Education and the State since 1850* (Manchester).

Baines, D. E. (1981) 'The Labour Supply and the Labour Market 1860–1914' in R. Floud and D. McCloskey, *The Economic History of Britain since 1700* (Cambridge).

Bamford, T. W. (1967) *The Rise of the Public Schools*.

Barnett, Correlli (1985) 'Long Term Industrial Performance in the United Kingdom: The Role of Education and Research 1850–1939' in D. J. Morris, *The Economic System in the United Kingdom* (Oxford).

(1986) *The Audit of War*.

Bell, Lady Florence (1907) *At the Works*.

Beloff, Michael (1968) *The Plateglass Universities*.

Bennet, Robert, Glennester, Howard and Nevison, Douglas (1993) *Learning Should Pay* (British Petroleum).

Berghoff H. (1990) 'Public Schools and the Decline of the British Economy 1870–1914', *Past and Present* no 129.

Berghoff H. and Moller R. (1994) 'Tired Pioneers and Dynamic Newcomers? A Comparative Essay on English and German entrepreneurial history 1870–1914' *Economic History Review* 47 no 2 May.

Best, Geoffrey (1975) 'Militarism and the Victorian Public School' in Brian Simon and Ian Bradley ed., *The Victorian Public School*.

Bishop T. H. J. H. and Wilkinson R. (1967) *Winchester and the Public School Elite*.

Broadberry S. N. and Crafts N. F. R. (1992) 'Britain's Productivity Gap in the 1930s: Some Neglected Factors', *Journal of Economic History* 52 no 3 September.

Burgess, Keith (1994) 'British Employers and Education Policy, 1934–45: A Decade of 'Missed Opportunities'?' *Business History* 36 no 6.

Cane, B. S. (1959) 'Scientific and Technical Subjects in the Curriculum of English Secondary Schools at the Turn of the Century', *British Journal of Educational Studies* November.

Cardwell, D. S. L. (1957) *The Organisation of Science in England.*

Cassells, Sir John (1990) *Britain's Real Skill Shortage and What to Do About It* (Policy Studies Institute).

Cassis, Y. (1985) 'Bankers in English Society in the late nineteenth century', *Economic History Review* 28 no 2 May.

Church, R. A. (1986) *The History of the British Coal Industry Vol. 3 1830–1913, Victorian Pre-eminence* (Oxford).

Coleman, D. C. (1973) 'Gentlemen and Players' *Economic History Review* 26 no 1 February.

Coleman D. C. and Macleod, Christine (1986) 'Attitudes to New Techniques: British Businessmen 1800–1950', *Economic History Review* 39 no 4 November.

Crowther, Sir Geoffrey (1959) *Fifteen to Eighteen, Report of the Central Advisory Council for Education* (HMSO).

Dean, D. W. (1970) 'H. A. L. Fisher, Reconstruction and Development of the 1918 Education Act', *British Journal of Educational Studies* October.

    (1971) 'Conservatism and the National Education System 1922–40', *Journal of Contemporary History* 6 no 2.

Dearle, N. B. (1914) *Industrial Training.*

Divall, Colin (1990) 'A Measure of Agreement: Employers and Engineering Studies in the Universities of England and Wales, 1897–1939', *Social Studies of Science* 20.

    (1991) 'Fundamental Science versus Design: Employers and Engineering Studies in British Universities 1935–1976', *Minerva* 29.

Douglas, J. W. B. (1964) *The Home and the School.*

Dunbabin, J. P. D. (1975) 'Oxford and Cambridge College Finances 1871–1913', *Economic History Review* 28 no 4 November.

Eason, M. (1996) 'Education and Training, the Key to Business Success? Human Resource Development at Thomas Firth and Sons Ltd *c.* 1880–1914', Papers of the Economic History Society Conference (University of Lancaster).

Edgerton, David (1996) *Science, Technology and the British Economic Decline 1870– 1970* (Cambridge).

Elbaum, Bernard (1991) 'The persistence of apprenticeship in Britain and its decline in the United States' in Gospel, Howard, *Industrial Training and Technological Innovation.*

Engel, A. J. (1983) *From Clergyman to Don, the Rise of the Academic Profession in Nineteenth Century Oxford* (Oxford).

    (1978) 'Oxford College Finances 1871–1913, a comment', *Economic History Review* 31 no 3 August.

Erickson, Charlotte (1959) *British Industrialists, Steel and Hosiery 1850–1950* (Cambridge).

Evans, Eric and Summerfield, Penny (1990) *Technical Education and the State since 1850* (Manchester).

Evans, E. W. and Wiseman, N. C. (1984) 'Education, Training and Economic Performance: British Economists' Views 1868–1939', *Journal of European Economic History, Spring.*

Eyre, J. Vargas (1958) *Henry Edward Armstrong 1848–1937.*

Finegold, David and Soskice, David (1988) 'The Failure of Training in Britain: Analysis and Prescription', *Oxford Review of Economic Policy* 4 no 3.

Fitzgerald, Robert (1993) 'Industrial Training and Management in Britain' in Kawabe, N., and Daito, E. *Education and Training in the Development of the Modern Corporation* (Tokyo).

Floud, J. E., Halsey, A. H. and Martin, F. M. (1956) *Social Class and Educational Opportunity.*

Floud, Roderick (1982) 'Technical Education and Economic Performance in Britain 1850–1914', *Albion.*

 (1984) 'Technical Education 1850–1914: Speculations on Human Capital Formation' (CEPR Discussion Paper no 12).

Foden, Frank (1970) *Philip Magnus, Victorian Educational Pioneer.*

Gray, J. L. and Moshinsky, Pearl (1935) 'Ability and Opportunity in English Education', *Sociological Review* 27 no. 2.

Goodman, Alissa, Johnson, Paul and Webb, Steven (1997) *Inequality in the United Kingdom* (IFS, Oxford).

Gospel, Howard F. (1991) *Industrial Training and Technological Innovation.*

 (1993a) *Whatever Happened to Apprenticeship Training in Britain?* University of Kent Studies in Economics No 93/14 September.

 (1993b) *Whatever Happened to Apprenticeship Training? A British, American, Australian comparison.* University of Kent Studies in Economics no 93/15 September.

Gray, H. B. and Turner, S. (1916) *Eclipse or Empire?*

Green, A. and Steedman, H. (1993) *Educational Provision, Educational Attainment and the Needs of Industry* (London, NIESR).

Guagnini, Anna (1993) 'Worlds apart, academic instruction and professional qualifications in the training of mechanical engineers in England 1850–1914' in Fox, Robert and Guagnini, Anna eds., *Education, Technology and Industrial Performance in Europe 1850–1939* (Cambridge).

Habbakuk, H. J. (1962) *British and American Technology in the Nineteenth Century* (Cambridge).

Halsey, A. H., Heath, A. F., Ridge, J. M. (1980) *Origins and Destinations. Family Class and Education in Modern Britain* (Oxford).

Hannah, Leslie (1987) 'Human Capital', *Oxford Review of Education* 13 no 2.

Harris, Jose (1993) *Private Lives, Public Spirit: Britain 1870–1914.*

Harrison, Brian, ed. (1994) *The History of the University of Oxford, Vol III The Twentieth Century* (Oxford).

Harvey, Charles and Press, Jon (1989) 'Overseas Investment and the Professional Advance of British Mining Engineers 1851–1914', *Economic History Review* 42 no 1 February.

Hennock, Peter (1990) 'Technological Education in England 1850–1926, the uses of a German model' *History of Education* 19 no 4.

Heward, Christine M (1988) *To Make a Man of Him.*

Hilken, T. J. N. (1967) *Engineering at Cambridge 1783–1965* (Cambridge).

Hogg, Ethel (1904) *Quintin Hogg: a Biography.*

Honey, J. R. de S. (1977) *Tom Brown's Universe, the Development of the Victorian Public School.*

(1987) 'The Sinews of Society, the Public Schools as a System' in Muller, D.K., Ringer, F. and Simon, B. ed., *The Rise of the Modern Educational System* (Cambridge).

Howarth, Janet (1987) 'Science Education in late-Victorian Oxford: A Curious Case of Failure?', *English Historical Review* 102.

Hudson, D. and Luckhurst K. W. (1954) *The Royal Society of Arts 1754–1954.*

Hutton, Will (1995) *The State We're In.*

James, Harold (1990) 'German Experience and the Myth of British Cultural Exceptionalism' in Collins, B and Robbins, K., *British Culture and Economic Decline.*

Jenkins H., and Jones, D.C. (1950) 'Social Class of Cambridge University Alumni of the Eighteenth and Nineteenth Centuries', *British Journal of Sociology* I.

Jeremy, D. J. (1984) 'Anatomy of the British Business Elite 1860–1980', *Business History* 26.

Johnson, Paul (1994) *Twentieth Century Britain, Economic, Social and Cultural Change.*

Jones, Ian (1988) 'An Evaluation of YTS', *Oxford Review of Economic Policy* 4 no 3.

Jones, M. J. (1997) 'The Agricultural Depression, Collegiate Finances, and the provision of Education at Oxford, 1871–1913', *Economic History Review* 50 no 1 February.

Kaser, M.C. (1966) 'Education and Economic Progress: Experience in Industrialized Market Economies' in Robinson, E. A. G and Vaizey, J., *The Economics of Education* (Cambridge).

Keeble, Shirley (1992) *The Ability To Manage, A Study of British Management 1890–1990* (Manchester).

Knox, William (1986) 'Apprenticeship and Deskilling in Britain 1850–1914', *International Review of Social History* 31, 1986 pt 2.

Krumpe, Elizabeth C. (1987) *The Educational Ideas of the Clarendon Headmasters 1860–1914* (New York).

Landes, David (1969) *The Unbound Prometheus* (Cambridge).

Le Guillon, Michael (1981) 'Technical Education 1850–1914' in Roderick G. and Stephens, M.D., *Where Did We Go Wrong?* (Lewes).

Little A. and Westergaard, J. (1964) 'The Trend of Class Differentials in Educational Opportunity in England and Wales', *British Journal of Sociology*.

Locke, Robert R. (1984) *The End of the Practical Man, Entrepreneurship and Higher Education in Germany, France and Great Britain 1880–1940* (Greenwich, Connecticut).

(1989) *Management and Higher Education since 1940* (Cambridge).

Lowe, R. (1983) 'The Expansion of Higher Education in England' in K. H. Jarausch, *The Transformation of Higher Learning 1860–1930* (Chicago).

Lowndes, G. A. N. (1969) *The Silent Social Revolution 1895–1965* (Oxford).

Lundgreen, P. (1975) 'Industrialisation and the Educational Formation of Manpower in Germany', *Journal of Social History* 9 no 1 Fall.

(1984) 'Education for the Science Based Industrial State? The Case for Nineteenth-Century Germany', *History of Education* 3 no 1.

Magnus, Sir Philip (1910) *Educational Aims and Efforts 1880–1910*.

Mangan, J. A. (1981) *Athleticism in the Victorian and Edwardian Public School* (Cambridge).

Matthews, R. C. O., Feinstein, C. H. and Odling Smee J. C. (1982) *British Economic Growth 1856–1973* (Oxford).

McClelland, Keith (1990) 'The transmission of collective knowledge: apprenticeship in engineering and shipbuilding 1850–1914' in Summerfield, Penny and Evans, Eric., *Technical Education and the State since 1850* (Manchester).

McCloskey, D. N. (1973) *Economic Maturity and Entrepreneurial Decline: British Iron and Steel 1870–1913* (Harvard).

McCormick, Kevin (1986) 'The Search for Corporatist Structures in British Higher Technological Education: the Creation of the National Advisory Council on Education in Industry and Commerce in 1948', *British Journal of Sociology of Education* 7 no 3.

McCulloch, Gary (1989) *The Secondary Technical School, a Usable Past?* (Lewes).

McCulloch, Gary, Jenkins, Edgar and Layton, David (1985) *Technological Revolution? the Politics of School Science and Technology in England and Wales since 1945* (Lewes).

Meadows, A. J. and Brock, W. H. (1975) 'Topics fit for Gentlemen, the Problem of Science in the Public School Curriculum' in Simon, Brian and Bradley, Ian., *The Victorian Public School*.

Millis, C. T. (1925) *Technical Education, its Development and Aims*.

Mitch, David, (1986) 'The Impact of Subsidies to Elementary Schooling on Enrolment Rates in Nineteenth Century England', *Economic History Review* 39 no 3 August.

  (1992) *The Rise of Popular Literacy in Victorian England* (University of Pennsylvania).

More, C. V. (1980) *Skill and the English Working Class 1870–1914*.

Musgrave, P. W. (1967) *Technical Change, the Labour Force and Education* (Oxford).

National Commission on Education (1995) *Learning to Succeed, the Way Ahead*.

Nicholas, Stephen (1985) 'Technical Education and the Decline of Britain 1870–1914' in Inkster, Ian ed., *The Steam Intellect Societies* (Nottingham).

O'Keefe, Dennis J. (1975) 'Some Economic Aspects of Raising the School Leaving Age in England and Wales in 1947', *Economic History Review* 28 no. 3 August.

Payne, Peter (1990) 'Entrepreneurship and British Economic Decline' in Collins, Bruce, and Robbins, Keith, *British Culture and Economic Decline*.

Pollard, Sidney (1983) *The Development of the British Economy 1914–1980*.

  (1989) *Britain's Prime and Britain's Decline 1870–1914*.

Prais, S. J. (1985) 'What Can We Learn from the German System of Education and Vocational Training?' in G. D. N. Worswick (ed.), *Education and Economic Performance* (Aldershot).

Prais, S. J. and K. Wagner (1983) *Schooling Standards in Britain and Germany, some Summary Comparisons Bearing on Economic Efficiency* (NIESR Discussion Paper 60, Industry Series 14).

Rae, John (1981) *The Public School Revolution, Britain's Independent Schools 1964–79*.

Raven, James (1989) 'British History and the Enterprise Culture', *Past and Present* 123 May.

Reader, W. J. (1966) *Professional Men*.

Reeder, D. (1987) 'The Reconstruction of Secondary Education in England 1869–1920' in Muller, D., Ringer, F. and Simon, B., *The Rise of the Modern Educational System 1870–1920* (Cambridge).

Renold, C. G. (1928) 'The Nature and Present Position of Skill in Industry', *Economic Journal*, December.

Robertson, P. L. (1974) 'Technical Education in the British Shipbuilding and Marine Engineering Industries 1863–1914', *Economic History Review* 27 no 2 May.

(1981) 'Employers and Engineering Education in Britain and the United States 1890–1914', *Business History* 23 March.

(1984) 'Scottish Universities and Industry 1860–1914' *Scottish Economic and Social History* 4.

(1990) 'The Development of an Urban University: Glasgow 1860–1914', *History of Education Quarterly* 30 no 1 Spring.

Robbins, L. (Lord) (1963) *Higher Education* Cmnd 2154, (HMSO).

Robinson, Peter (1997) *Literacy, Numeracy and Economic Performance* (Centre for Economic Performance).

Roderick G. W. and Stephens M. D. (1972) *Scientific and Technical Education in Nineteenth Century England* (Newton Abbott).

(1972) *Education and Industry in the Nineteenth Century*.

(1974) 'Scientific Studies and Scientific Manpower in the English Civic Universities 1870–1914', *Science Studies* 4 no 1.

(1976) 'Scientific Studies at Oxford and Cambridge 1850–1914', *British Journal of Educational Studies*, February.

(1982) 'The British Educational System 1870–1970' in Roderick, G. W. and Stephens M. D. eds., *The British Malaise, Industrial Performance, Education and Training in Britain Today* (Lewes).

Rose, Jonathan (1993) 'Willingly to School: the Working Class Response to Elementary Education in Britain 1875–1918' *Journal of British Studies* 32 April.

Rose, Mary (1994) 'Investment in Human Capital and British Manufacturing Industry to 1990' in Kirby, Maurice W. and Rose, Mary, *Business Enterprise in Modern Britain*.

Rothblatt, Sheldon (1968) *The Revolution of the Dons, Cambridge and Society in Victorian England*.

Rubinstein, David (1969) *School Attendance in London 1870–1904* (Hull).

Rubinstein, W. D. (1986) 'Education and Social Origins of British Elites 1880– 1970', *Past and Present* 112, August.

(1993) 'Education, the Gentleman and British Entrepreneurship' in W. D. *Rubinstein, Capitalism, Culture and Decline in Britain 1750–1900*.

Saint, Andrew (1989) 'Technical Education in the Early LCC' in Saint, Andrew *Politics and the People of London*.

Sandberg, Lars. G. (1982) 'Ignorance, Poverty and Economic Backwardness,' *The Journal of European Economic History no. 3 Winter*.

Sanderson, Michael (1972) *The Universities and British Industry 1850–1970*.

(1978) 'The Professor as Industrial Consultant, Oliver Arnold and the British Steel Industry 1900–1914', *Economic History Review* 31 no 4 November.

(1987) *Educational Opportunity and Social Change in England*.

(1991) 'Social Equity and Industrial Need: a Dilemma of English

Education since 1945' in Gourvish T.R. and O'Day A., *Britain Since 1945.*

(1994) *The Missing Stratum, Technical School Education in England 1900–1990s.*

(1996) 'French Influences on Technical and Managerial Education in England 1870–1940' in Cassis, Y., Crouzet, F., and Gourvish, T. R., *Management and Business in Britain and France* (Oxford).

(1997) 'The English Public Schools and the Economic Depression of the 1930s' in Lanthier, Pierre and Watelat, Hubert, *Private Enterprise during Economic Crises: Tactics and Strategies* (New York, Ottawa, Toronto).

(1998) 'Education and Economic Decline 1870–1914 – an innocent suspect?' in Dormois J-P and McCloskey D., *The British Industrial Decline Revisited.*

Seaborne, Malcolm (1968) 'Education in the Nineties, the Work of the Technical Education Committees' in Simon, Brian, ed., *Education in Leicestershire* (Leicester).

Sheldrake J. and Vickerstaff, S. (1987) *The History of Industrial Training in Britain* (Aldershot).

Sherington, Geoffrey (1981) *English Education, Social Change and War 1911–1920* (Manchester).

Shrosbree, Colin (1988) *Public Schools and Private Education* (Manchester).

Silver, Harold (1983) 'Expectations of Higher Education' in *Education as History.*

Smithers, Alan, and Robinson, Pamela (1992) *Technology in the National Curriculum* (London, The Engineering Council).

Springhall, John (1994) 'Disseminating Impure Literature, the 'Penny Dreadful' Publishing Business since 1860' *Economic History Review* 47 no 3 August.

Stanworth, Philip (1980) 'Trade, Gentility and Upper Class Education in Victorian Britain', *International Studies of Management and Organisation* 10 nos 1–2.

Stone, Lawrence (1969) 'Literacy and Education in England 1640–1900', *Past and Present* 42, February.

(1974) 'The Size and Composition of the Oxford Student Body 1580–1910' in Lawrence Stone ed. *The University in Society*, vol. 1 *Oxford and Cambridge from the Fourteenth to the Early Nineteenth Centuries* (Princeton).

Supple, Barry (1994), 'Fear of Failing: Economic History and the Decline of Britain', *Economic History Review* 47 no 3, August.

Symonds, Richard (1986) *Oxford and Empire: The Last Lost Cause.*

Szreter, Simon (1997) 'British Economic Decline and Human Resources' in Clarke, Peter and Trebilcock, Clive, *Understanding Decline* (Cambridge).

Temin, Peter (1966) 'The Relative Decline of the British Steel Industry 1880–1913' in Rosovsky, Henry ed., *Industrialisation in Two Systems* (Harvard).

Thistlethwaite, Frank (1996) *A Lancashire Family Inheritance* (Cambridge).

Tomlinson, Jim (1996) 'Inventing 'Decline': The Falling behind of the British Economy in the Post War Years' *Economic History Review* 49 no 4 November.

Venables, Sir Peter (1978) *Higher Education Developments: the Technological Universities*.

Vincent, David (1989), *Literacy and Popular Culture in England 1750–1914* (Cambridge).

Vlaeminke, Meriel (1990) 'The Subordination of Technical Education in Secondary Schooling 1870–1914' in Summerfield, Penny and Evans, Eric, *Technical Education and the State since 1850* (Manchester).

Walford, Geoffrey and Miller, Henry (1991) *City Technology College* (Milton Keynes).

Ward, David (1967) 'The Public Schools and Industry in Britain after 1870', *Journal of Contemporary History* 2 no 3.

Weinberg, Ian (1967) *The English Public Schools* (New York).

West, E. G. (1975) 'Educational Slowdown and Public Intervention in Nineteenth Century England: a Study in the Economics of Bureaucracy', *Explorations in Economic History* 12.

Wiener, Martin J. (1981) *English Culture and the Decline of the Industrial Spirit 1850–1980* (Cambridge).

Wilkinson, Rupert (1964) *The Prefects* (Oxford).

Wolf, Alison (1997) *GNVQs 1993–97, a National Survey Report*.

Wooldridge, Adrian (1990) *Education and the Labour Market, an English Disaster* (London, Social Market Foundation).

(1994) *Measuring the Mind* (Cambridge).

Wrigley, Julia (1986) 'Technical Education and Industry in the Nineteenth Century' in Elbaum, B. and Lazonick W., *The Decline of the British Economy* (Oxford).

(1982) 'The Division between Mental and Manual Labor: Artisan Education in Science in Nineteenth Century Britain' in *American Journal of Sociology* 88 Supplement.

Index

New Studies in Economic and Social History

Titles in the series available from Cambridge University Press

Previously published as

Studies in Economic and Social History

Titles in the series available from the Macmillan Press Limited

Economic History Society

The Economic History Society, which numbers around 3,000 members, publishes the *Economic History Review* four times a year (free to members) and holds an annual conference.

Enquiries about membership should be addressed to

The Assistant Secretary
Economic History Society
PO Box 70
Kingswood
Bristol
BS15 5TB

Full time students may join at special rates.